Sociology and Education in the Indian Context

SOCIOLOGY AND EDUCATION IN THE INDIAN CONTEXT

Editor

V. C. Pandey

ISHA BOOKS
DELHI-110 033

Sociology and Education in the Indian Context

ISBN: 81-8205-152-5

Published in 2007 in India by
Isha Books,
B-63, Ist Floor, New Gupta Colony,
Near DDA Market, Delhi-110 009
Phone : 9212142040
Email : ishabooks@hotmail.com
Laser Typesetting at: Shree Vaishnavi Creations, Delhi
Printed at: Rajdhani Printers, Delhi

PREFACE

As our society is becoming more and more complex day by day due to the trends of modernisation, urbanisation, secularisation, globalisation etc, new problems of education are coming into focus. It is in this context that new researches in sociology of education are called for. Though a good deal of development has taken place in sociology of education in Western Countries, in India much less work has been accomplished in this field. Studies are available regarding only some facets of education in India. Sociologists, social psychologists as well as educationists have mainly contributed to these studies.

This comprehensive work lays down the basic concepts of sociological foundations of education in Indian context as required to be understood by every specialist of the subject. It lays down the fundamentals of education required to be understood by every scholar and student of the subject alike. The emphasis has been laid on the nature of educational sociology, education and society, education in Indian social context, social mobility, child's socialisation, social change, social control, culture and place of family, community, social values, modernisation as well as religious and moral values in education. It will definitely provide invaluable guidance to young educational researchers and teachers.

Editor

CONTENTS

1

SOCIOLOGICAL BASIS OF EDUCATION

The idea of sociology (including social anthropology) in a regional context has several meanings:

1. ethnographic or sociological knowledge of the region, cultivated not only by scholars belonging to the region but also by those from other regions in India and/or other countries in the world, which may be available in English as well as in the regional language;
2. sociological literature only in the regional language;
3. sociology cultivated only by scholars belonging to the region, in English as well as in the regional language; and
4. development of sociological institutions in the region, including research and teaching carried out there, whether regional in orientation or not.

The history of sociology in Gujarat may be divided into three phases. The first phase began roughly in the middle of the 19th century and ended in about 1920. During this phase, although there was no formal teaching and research under the name of sociology, considerable literature of a sociological nature was published both in Gujarati and in English. It saw the publication of the Gujarat volumes of The Bombay Gazetteer, based on a massive exercise by British officials to collect information about various aspects of society and culture. Of these volumes, the one on Gujarat population, actually on castes, tribes, and so on, was translated into Gujarati.

Similarly, A.K. Forbes, a British official turned scholar, wrote his monumental book, *Rasmala*, covering many aspects of history, myths, society and culture of Gujarat. He influenced a number of local scholars to write nibandhs (essays) in Gujarati on various aspects of life, such as caste, famines, ghosts, women's manners, etc. All this literature can be read with profit even today. The second phase in the development of sociology in Gujarat began with the establishment of the Department of Sociology in Bombay University in 1920 and ended around 1950. The first professor and head of the department was Patrick Geddes but he soon left and was succeeded by the legendary G.S. Ghurye. His junior colleague was N.A. Thooti, a Parsi, who wrote, The Vaishnavas of Gujarat.

Coterminous with the establishment of the Bombay department, Alan Widgery, professor of philosophy in Baroda College, planned to start research in sociology, and as part of this effort he brought out The Indian Journal of Sociology in 1920, perhaps the first sociological journal to be published in India. Unfortunately the journal did not survive beyond the first volume. However, a certain consciousness of sociology seems to have developed in Gujarat; a few students from Gujarat went to study sociology at Bombay University - the best known being K.M. Kapadia, I.P. Desai and A.R. Desai. This phase also saw the publication of literature based on censuses conducted in the British as well as the Baroda state territories and the literature on castes and tribes. This genre of literature for Baroda state, published under the editorship of G.H. Desai, is superior to that for the British territory.

The Baroda state also published an excellent report on The Hindu Joint Family: Its Economic and Social Aspects by N.C. Desai in 1936. The teaching of sociology began for the first time towards the end of this phase - in 1946 - at the undergraduate level at Shamaldas College, Bhavnagar with the appointment of I.P. Desai as lecturer. He stayed there till 1951, when K.R. Unni succeeded him. They taught the subject according to the syllabus framed under Ghurye's leadership, because all colleges in Gujarat were affiliated to Bombay University. A new phase in the development of sociology began in Gujarat, as everywhere else in India, with Independence. The most important part of it was the establishment of new universities and of new departments of sociology.

The first of these was the department in Maharaja Sayajirao University of Baroda established in 1951 and next, the department in Gujarat University, Ahmedabad established in 1954. Other departments followed gradually, namely, at the South Gujarat, North Gujarat, Saurashtra, Bhavnagar, and Sardar Patel universities. Six of these seven universities, plus the SNDT University for Women in Mumbai, have more than 100 affiliated colleges teaching sociology mainly at the undergraduate level. In addition, there is a small department of social anthropology in Gujarat Vidyapeeth, a deemed university. The sociology department in Baroda University has been different for three main reasons.

1. This university is unitary in its constitution and therefore the teaching for all the programmes - BA, MA and Ph.D - is done under the same roof; in other universities the teaching for BA is done in affiliated colleges and the teaching for MA and Ph.D is done in the university department, barring a few colleges recognised for MA teaching. Consequently, in Baroda there is greater integration between the teaching done at the three levels, and the undergraduate students have the advantage of being taught by junior as well as senior teachers.
2. All teaching is in English in Baroda, while there has been a gradual shift from English to Gujarati in other universities. Consequently, the Baroda department has been more cosmopolitan in recruitment of teachers as well as students and in its general orientation to teaching and research.
3. The Baroda department grew under the leadership of two stalwarts, first M.N. Srinivas and then I.P. Desai.

At the time of its establishment, Baroda University decided, just as Poona University had decided two or three years earlier and several other universities were to do later, that it would adopt the syllabi of Bombay University till such time as it was able to frame its own. Bombay University was the only university teaching sociology in all of western India since 1920 - first under the leadership of Geddes and then Ghurye. It is well known that Ghurye combined in himself three intellectual traditions of his time on account of his training in these traditions: first, sanskrit and Indology; second, sociology under Hobhouse at London School of Economics; and third, anthropology under W.H.R. Rivers at Cambridge.

Srinivas studied sociology under Ghurye and then anthropology under Radcliffe-Brown and Evans-Pritchard at Oxford. Both Ghurye and Srinivas subsumed anthropology under sociology. Since Srinivas joined Baroda University at the beginning of the academic session 1951-52, he had to teach according to the syllabus of Bombay University. The subsidiary subject of anthropology, which the department started teaching first, consisted of two papers - social anthropology and material culture, both to be taught over a period of two years. Srinivas began with social anthropology. The syllabus required it to be taught with reference to three textbooks: Ruth Benedict's *Patterns of Culture*, Goldenweiser's *Anthropology*, and R.H. Lowie's *Primitive Religion*.

However, Srinivas rejected all these textbooks, which in effect meant rejecting the textbooks chosen by Ghurye. In their place Srinivas prescribed Evans-Pritchard's Social Anthropology, Firth's Human Types, and Radcliffe-Brown's unpublished manuscript, 'Method in Social Anthropology', a copy of which Radcliffe-Brown had given him in Oxford and which he edited and published in 1959. He also asked the students to review two small books: Evans-Pritchard's Divine Kingship among the Shilluk and Verrier Elwin's Indian Aboriginals. His prescription of these textbooks was informal.

No other teacher or head of department could have dared to so violate university statutes and ordinances, but Srinivas' ability to do so arose out of the close support he enjoyed from

Vice Chancellor, Hansa Mehta and Pro Vice Chancellor, A.R. Wadia. Srinivas refused to yield to pressures to start the MA programme in the first year itself, but began to enrol students for the Ph.D programme. They all came from allied disciplines: three lecturers from the faculty of social work, one research assistant in the department of archaeology and ancient Indian culture, and one student with M.Sc in anthropology from Delhi University, Y.V.S. Nath. Nath was also appointed as research assistant and a little later as lecturer. This as well as other appointments showed that Srinivas did not follow the distinction between sociology and anthropology in making appointments.

Along with the recruitment of research students, Srinivas began to organise research seminars, a novelty in Baroda at that time. He also began to implement his preference for field research in the first year itself, asking all his research students to do fieldwork. He himself went on a field trip to Rampura for two months in May-June 1952, in continuation of his earlier long spell of fieldwork there. The academic year 1952-53 was marked by two major events: the appointment of I.P. Desai as reader, and the launching of a new syllabus for BA (Hons.) in sociology. Desai had by this time moved from Bhavnagar to Deccan College, Poona. He was a classmate and friend of Srinivas in Bombay, but his orientation was different. He had done his Ph.D on 'Crime and Society' on the basis of library materials.

However, he had carried out a study of high school students in Poona on the basis of a questionnaire. While Srinivas and Desai differed in techniques of research, they agreed on a strong empirical foundation for social studies. The new BA (Hons.) syllabus represented a fusion of sociology and social anthropology under the rubric of sociology, perhaps the first such undergraduate syllabus in India. It also represented a fusion of the approaches of Srinivas and Desai. The department could not frame its own syllabus for MA for four years and the students had therefore to study according to the Bombay University syllabus. Not only that, the department offered to teach only four out of eight papers in sociology and the students had thus to choose four papers in some other subject.

The four papers in sociology were general sociology, Indian sociology, social psychology, and social biology. Social biology included mainly the study of race, racism and eugenics. This was Ghurye's way of co-opting physical anthropology into sociology. For the paper on general sociology the students had to read the books prescribed in the Bombay syllabus, namely, Society by McIver and Page, and Sociology by Ginsberg. To these was added Structure and Function in Primitive Society by Radcliffe-Brown at Srinivas' suggestion. For Indian sociology the students were asked to read Caste and Class in India by Ghurye, Marriage and Family in India by Kapadia, and Hindu Social Organisation by Prabhu. The MA examination was held at the end of two years. Both because of this and because of a shortage of teachers, the students of the first and the second year were taught together.

The entire examination was covered in just a few days. Usually the questions required essay type answers. The candidates were asked to answer not more than three questions and the paper was evaluated as a whole, so that one could answer less than three questions and yet get full marks. This method of examination encouraged selective reading. Like the BA syllabus the new MA syllabus reflected fusion of sociology and social anthropology. Once these syllabi were in place, the department was poised for growth. The number of students in the BA, MA and Ph.D courses increased steadily and the department earned a reputation for attracting bright students.

During the eight years that Srinivas worked in the department, there were 14 active Ph.D students, eight under his supervision and six under I.P. Desai's. They worked on varied themes: castes and tribes, factories, different levels of education, journalism, sociology of development, social reforms, historical sociology, and so on. They published high quality papers in reputed journals. Most of the dissertations were published, and all well received. These students came from several different parts of India and fanned out later to occupy important academic positions all over the country. Within a short period of time the department attracted national and international attention.

A number of scholars from India and abroad visited the department and gave seminars and lectures. Its publications received worldwide acclaim. Around 1958 the University Grants Commission, impressed by its work, sanctioned generous grants for faculty positions, fellowships, scholarships, fieldwork, and a separate building. Throughout the period of Srinivas' and Desai's headship of the department, a policy of subsuming anthropology under sociology was followed in every sphere of activity. Clearly, this was in continuation of Ghurye's policy which was visible all over western India where his students occupied leadership positions. The only exception was Poona. Anthropology was given a separate status at the Deccan College Postgraduate and Research Institute.

Irawati Karve, a one-time student of Ghurye's, who headed the anthropology department, subsumed sociology under it, although sociology eventually became a separate department. Otherwise none of the many universities that were established in Gujarat and Maharashtra after Independence set up a separate department of anthropology. Srinivas left Baroda to join Delhi University in early 1959. I.P. Desai's elevation as professor and head of the department was merely a formality. The department worked on an even keel for some time under his leadership. But the period of decline began around 1961 and there was a large scale exodus of teachers and students from the department. Finally I.P Desai too left in 1966. For nearly 25 years the department remained in poor shape. It is only recently that it has once again started looking up.

There has been a phenomenal growth in the numbers of sociology students and teachers in the undergraduate colleges after Independence. There were about 13,000 students and 140 teachers in about 60 colleges at this level in 1988-89, according to B.V. Shah's survey. Since the number of colleges has now gone up to about 100, the number of teachers and students must have gone up proportionately. Sociology here is taught almost entirely in Gujarati.

The college teachers, forming the largest segment of the community of sociology teachers, have contributed very little to creation of sociological knowledge even in Gujarati, leave alone in English. Their transmission of sociological knowledge too is not impressive. Their teaching has suffered due to the vicious circle of non-challenging syllabi, heavy teaching loads, absence of original textbooks and dominance of guide books, lack of library resources, widespread resort to coaching classes, and the politics of boards of studies and examinations. The syllabi are not revised for years to accommodate fresh knowledge available even in Gujarati.

The condition of teaching at the MA level, which is usually done in the university departments, is somewhat better. At least the syllabi are impressive. But a large part of the syllabus does not get taught because most students are unable to read books prescribed in English. An increasing number of postgraduate teachers seem ill-equipped to transmit the vast storehouse of sociological knowledge available in English. The medium of teaching at M.Phil and Ph.D has also gradually shifted from English to Gujarati. Of about 60 M.Phil dissertations done so far at Gujarat, South Gujarat, and Saurashtra universities, eight have been in English and the rest in Gujarati.

Similarly, of about 64 Ph.D dissertations done at Gujarat, South Gujarat, Saurashtra, and Sardar Patel universities, 11 are in English and the rest in Gujarati. The market for research books in Gujarati is small, commercial publishers are not interested in publishing Ph.D dissertations. Institutional subsidies are also few. Moreover, little effort is made to make the results of good dissertations available in the form of papers in Gujarati journals, let alone in English. Consequently, a great deal of new knowledge remains unknown to the scholarly public.To what extent the teachers in postgraduate departments are involved in creative research is also questionable. There was a strong tradition among the first generation of teachers like Taraben Patel, B.V. Shah and Vimal P. Shah that a university teacher should teach as well do research. This tradition has gradually weakened.

While the role of universities in pursuing qualitatively significant sociological research has been declining, a few autonomous research institutions have been playing an increasingly important role in this respect. The leading institution is the Centre for Social Studies in Surat, founded by the late I.P. Desai in 1966 and supported by grants from the Indian Council of Social Science Research and the Government of Gujarat. Successive bands of dedicated scholars there have contributed a large number of studies on a variety of themes connected mainly with Gujarat.

The centre has published books and papers, produced project reports both in Gujarati and English, organised seminars, and performed several other academic functions with distinction. It also publishes a Gujarati journal, Arthat. A few other institutions have also played a small though significant role.A Gujarat Sociological Association has been in existence since 1988, and it organizes conferences from time to time. Most of the papers and discussions there have been in Gujarati. In the main, sociological studies in Gujarat have increasingly tended to be oriented towards Gujarat and are in the Gujarati medium. This orientation is perfectly legitimate and should be respected, but its quality remains a matter of concern.

There have been some excellent studies in Gujarati, but they are exceptions. Most studies suffer from some serious limitations. First, the studies are non-incremental. That is to say, they do not follow the goal of establishing even all-Gujarat propositions, let alone all-India ones. Usually each study stands isolated on its own. The authors make no attempt to compare their work with available works even in Gujarati and to carry forward an argument or an observation critically. Second, there is a lack of understanding of diversities within Gujarati society and culture and, therefore, lack of concern for building up a systematic comparative sociology of Gujarat. Third, there is an absence of terminological, conceptual, methodological and theoretical rigour. This limitation arises mainly out of the inability to use English as a library language.

Soon after Srinivas came to Baroda he reviewed the sociological literature on Gujarat and wrote a significant paper, 'Prospects of Sociological Research in Gujarat'. It is high time another serious, critical retrospective is attempted and new prospects envisioned. This will require a genuinely integrated view of sociology and social anthropology which Srinivas had adopted and which unfortunately has weakened after he left Baroda University. Regionalisation of sociology and social anthropology in all the linguistic regions of India seems to be an inevitable process. It needs to be accepted as a fact.

From time immemorial, India has been a centre for learning. Thousands of years ago, great scholars used to teach through the scriptures. A variety of subjects such as philosophy, religion, medicine, literature, drama and arts, astrology, mathematics and sociology were taught and masterpieces on these subjects have been written. Under the Buddhist influence, education was available to virtually everyone who wanted it and some world famous institutions arose out of the monasteries, such as, Nalanda, Vikramshila and Takshashila. Nalanda is especially noteworthy, flourishing from 5th to 13th century AD. It had at one time about ten thousand resident students and teachers on its roll, which included Chinese, Sri Lankan, Korean and other international scholars.

During the 11th century, the Muslims established elementary and secondary schools, "Madrassahs" or colleges and even universities at cities like Delhi, Lucknow and Allahabad, using Arabic mostly as the medium of instruction. During the mediaeval period, there was excellent interaction between Indian and Islamic traditions in all fields of knowledge, like theology, religion, philosophy, fine arts, painting, architecture, mathematics, medicine and astronomy. With the arrival of the British, English education came into being with the help of the

European missionaries. In 1817, Hindu College was established in Calcutta. The Elphinstone Institution was set up in 1834 in Bombay.

In 1857 three universities were set up at Calcutta, Madras and Bombay. Since then, Western education has made steady advances in the country. With 226 universities and thousands of colleges affiliated to them, 428 Engineering colleges and technological institutes, more than a 100 medical colleges, scores of agricultural institutes and many other specialized centres of learning and research in every subject and discipline, India can claim its position as one of the leading countries providing quality higher education to its people as well as to students and scholars coming from countries all over the world. Indian universities and institutes of higher education and research today have made a significant contribution to transmission of knowledge and enquiry into frontiers of science and technology.

In the field of traditional subjects of arts and humanities as well as in pure sciences, applied physics and chemistry, mathematics and in areas of technology, the universities and higher institutes have been playing a leading role to transform the country into a modern industrialized, technologically advanced state. The ushering of green revolution and tremendous progress in dairy development have made India a major food-producing country on one hand; on the other hand, its development of space technology, production and launching of indigenous satellites, development of peaceful nuclear energy have brought it into the forefront of technologically advanced nations to which a large number of developing countries looks for training and guidance.

The Indian universities and institutes of higher learning have been playing their role to promote the needs and aspirations of higher education and research to Indian students and scholars. These centres have been extending their cooperation and friendship towards students of other developing countries also, where facilities for higher studies and research are not adequate. In addition, a number of overseas students are also drawn to Indian educational institutions providing high quality education at very competitive prices.

FUTURE VISION FOR EDUCATION

Despite rapid advances in industrial development, India is today still seen as a non-competitive labour oriented society. Two thirds of our work force is dependent on agriculture for a living. In most industrial sectors, competitive advantage is built around labour. A substantial part of our exports are in the form of labour intensive goods and services. In information technology, some flag our vast pool of labour as an advantage while others say that a majority of them are not working in cutting edge areas.

A number of economic reforms are hampered by their impact on labour and employment - be it privatisation of public enterprises, reduction in tariffs, moving to a quantitative regime or restraining wasteful government expenditure.

We have rigid labour laws that protect the interests of 300 lakhs employees in the government, public sector and organised private sector. The large numbers of workers in the unorganised sector and agriculture have no such protection. These labour laws hinder the creation of several hundred million new jobs that will be required for our growing population. Rigid labour laws are also hampering investments that have high employment elasticity, much needed by a populous nation. Labour related issues are centre stage in our current phase of reforms.

But, at the same time, the power of people in India is enormous. Imagine the potential for growth and development if over a billion people, one sixth of humanity, are educated, creative and enterprising. We have the numbers, but not the quality. Labour is both as a promise as well as a peril in Indian society.

In contrast, the developed world is shaping to be part of an information society. In such a society intellectual capital will be at a premium. Businesses in the information society will see employees work as quasi-owners in small cohesive organisations. Conventional models of employment that are labour oriented will be unable to unleash the human potential. Information intensive businesses will demand the nurture of creativity and innovation.

Organisations in the information society will tend to be smaller nuclear outfits rather than large monoliths. Traditionally organisations were designed for stability. In an information led world, organisations would be designed for change. Innovation will be at the heart of competitiveness in the information society. Innovation is a commitment to create future growth. Societies will tend to be research intensive. Already, R&D expenditures are 1.8% of GDP in Europe, 2.7% in USA and 2.8% in Japan and would tend to move higher in absolute and relative terms. Tighter patent laws will support the sustenance of such expenditures. Innovation without knowledge and people is unimaginable.

The information society will place emphasis on soft assets - programmes that run computer systems, systems solutions that integrate businesses, people who drive innovation and ideas that create the future. It will be a world where services will make up a significant component of economic value.

In such a society there will be much education occurring outside of schools. Education will draw on vastly more powerful technology. For example, learning through a two-way voice activated computer assisted self-paced learning. Learners will be able to go beyond the classroom. They will obtain information in a variety of forms - text, data, sound, video - from all over the world, at any time and at rapidly diminishing costs. Multimedia materials will reflect local values and culture, provide visual images of desired behaviour, collaborate across borders and access information not previously available. The information society will be education centric - in content, network, delivery and outcome.

As the world moves to forging an information society founded on education, India cannot remain behind as a non-competitive labour oriented society. India has to envision to being a competitive knowledge economy.

India has to create an environment that does not produce industrial workers and labourers but fosters knowledge workers. Such people must be at the cutting edge of knowledge, be competitive and innovative. Education development has a major role to play in shaping knowledge workers and, in turn, placing India in the vanguard in the information age.

While the larger world embraces the information age, the world of education in India encompasses different 'worlds' that live side by side. One world includes only a fortunate few with access to modern institutions, computers, Internet access and expensive overseas education. A second world wants to maintain status quo - teachers, administrators, textbook publishers, students - all have reasons to prefer things to remain as they are or change only gradually. The third world struggles with fundamental issues such as no books, wrong books, teachers desperately in need of training, teachers' with poor commitment, rote learning of irrelevant material, classrooms with hundred students, dirty floors and no toilets.

India cannot hope to succeed in the information age on the back of such three disparate worlds.

The imperative for India is to raise standards of the vast majority with poor education, break the education sector free from its inertia and forge a society that places knowledge as the cornerstone of its development.

At the same time, It is difficult to envisage the Indian society, with its ethos centred on family values and caring, being in a purely competitive mould. The tradition of co-operation and coexistence in India, among diverse communities, religions and languages and regions, has to be sustained.

Therefore, a vision for education in India has to inspire creation of a knowledge-based society, induce competitiveness yet foster a sense of co-operation. Thus, the vision for education in India would be "TO CREATE A COMPETITVE, YET CO-OPERATIVE, KNOWLEDGE BASED SOCIETY."

Objectives

Several strategic objectives would have to be pursued in order to realise this vision. These are:

- Provide quality primary education facilities to every citizen of India within a distance of one kilometre from his residence.
- Provide and support the private sector in the establishment of high quality secondary education facilities in every taluka.
- Encourage the establishment of world class higher education facilities at every district head quarters.
- Encourage the creation of state-of-the-art professional research based education institutions in all disciplines.
- Encourage institutes of education for physical education and education for the challenged.
- Integrate education with information and communication technologies to:
  - create smart schools,
  - network and deliver education and training,
  - institutionalise distance education,
- Create and maintain data bases, and continuously analyse trends.
- Develop human resources required for the education process.
- Continuously upgrade educational content in multiple media.

— Create institutional linkages to other sectors of social development such as health and rural development.
— Motivate non-resident Indians to participate in India's education programmes on a voluntary or sabbatical basis.
— Market India as a destination for affordable, high quality education.

Guiding Principles

The following guiding principles must permeate the pursuit of the above strategic objectives:

— Foster a healthy mix of state supported education with private initiatives.
— Costs of education must be affordable to the under privileged sections of society.
— Quality of education must be continuously monitored and upgraded to ensure high standards.
— User pays principle to be enforced strictly for higher education supported by loan schemes as well as financial grants for economically and socially backward sections of society.

Primary Education

Compulsory and free primary education must be on top of our education agenda. There is no getting away from enforcing the Constitutional commitment to compulsory education till the age of fourteen years, provided by Article 45 and reinforced by a historical Supreme court judgement declaring education as a fundamental right.

Compulsory and free primary education is feasible only through active involvement of local bodies at the panchayat and municipal levels. In our endeavour to enforce compulsory education, it must be recognised that an important reason for drop out, apart from economic factors, is that children feel inferior. In many cases parents feel inferior as well and consequently do not send children to school. If enrolment levels are to go up, every child has to see a school as unthreatening and stimulating.

Compulsory and free primary education will entail increased spending on education. This has to be met by restructuring of inter-sectoral allocations and divestment of loss making public sector companies. For example, the average annual plan expenditure on education (1992-97 plan) was Rs.3,920 crores and the annual losses of all state electricity boards (1997-98) was Rs.10,684 crores which is 2.72 times the average annual plan expenditure on education. There must be a political will and a conviction that compulsory and free primary education is an investment in India's future.

Equally, there is a case for free secondary education. However, this can be taken up once the primary education aspect is addressed and when primary level enrolments reach 95%, say by the year 2005, which is feasible.

Teaching

In the current system of education, the lack of opportunities for creativity for teachers as well as students is stifling. Preoccupation with textbooks and external examinations, to the exclusion of the process of education, is partly responsible for this. Whole generations of teachers have not known any other system and changes in the present system will meet with resistance. There is also an inertia in the system to upgrading educational material given cosy relationships between textbook writers, education administrators and publishers.

The government spends 90 to 97% of our total educational budget at primary and secondary levels on staff salaries. Studies undertaken by the National Teachers' Commission indicate that a majority of teachers are ill-prepared, do not keep abreast of developments in their disciplines and take private tutions at the cost of institutional work.

Training of teachers to infuse commitment, sensory learning, experiential learning, computer-aided teaching and technology led learning has to be the second item on the agenda for reforms. The Government of India and State Governments have to facilitate this process by bringing about regulations for continuous teacher quality upgradation.

A system of evaluation of teachers by students, at least in higher education , is due. At the primary and secondary levels, teachers must be made accountable for retention of children. These are revolutionary concepts in our current mindset and are bound to meet with stiff resistance. However, it has the potential to bring about high teaching standards.

Currently, undergraduate and postgraduate teaching have been put on par. This is disastrous. There must be a differentiation in teachers' education and experience based on levels of teaching.

Technology

The use of technology in the process of education comes third on the agenda. India has a unique opportunity to leapfrog in the use of technology in education. Our vast and growing resources in information technology and the social awareness of the benefits of information technology must be leveraged to bring about smart schools that integrate computers, networks and content.

Computers are becoming ubiquitous and computer literacy will be as important as literacy. In India, Internet made its debut in the mid-eighties as an educational and research network called ERNET. However, the early advantage was never capitalised. Computer education has to be an integral part of the curriculum from the school level.

The 'Class 2000' initiative of the Education Department to impart 'computer based' education in 100 smart schools, 'computer aided education' in 1000 schools and 'general computer literacy' in 10,000 schools is laudable. However, the effort has to be on a much larger scale. It has to be in the nature of a National Mission.

There should be at least one smart school in each district of India, which is completely networked. This should be implemented to cover all schools over the next five years. Private sector should be encouraged through tax benefits to invest heavily in this mission.

The use of satellite communication technology presents another great opportunity for primary education. India had an early start in the seventies and eighties in delivering higher level education to directly to homes, thanks to the work done by ISRO, UGC and Doordarshan. However, the low penetration of television could not bring about a revolution in distance education . Today, with the widespread use of television and the envisaged spread of high band optic fibre networks, the opportunity to use communications technology in education could have never been more appealing.

A concerted effort in supporting primary and secondary education through communications technology is an imperative. This has the benefit of cutting through the maze and inertia in the existing education system - ranging from poor access to facilities to absence of paid teachers in classrooms in rural schools.

Sensory Learning

The current education system in India is oriented to teaching. There is an emphasis on learning by rote from a very young age. Pre-school and primary education is obsessed with learning by reading and writing. These are relatively less developed faculties in children in the age group three to six. Ironically, learning by hearing and feeling, which are better developed faculties, are not given prominence. Child psychologists have repeatedly pointed out to this basic lacuna in primary education.

The emphasis on reading and writing from a very young age is also not conducive to creativity. The latent curiosity in children is not tapped.

Thus, an important agenda for reforms is to migrate from teaching to 'sensory learning' in order to provoke curiosity. Pre-school learning should not be allowed to degenerate into a formal learning. The accent must be on fostering creative joy and healthy psychological development. In the process, a strong foundation for an innovative society would be created.

Learning to Learn

The current system of book-based and theory-oriented teaching does not inculcate independent thinking. It should be changed to make the students learn by practice and experience. This should be initiated from the primary level of education.

In the information age, information would be available in multiple forms and through multiple media. Learning to learn from a vast array of information, instead of being taught, would be critical. The teacher's role has to transform to one of a facilitator. Such a shift from teaching to learning to learn would encourage the students to develop an innovative mindset from the very beginning, which is important in building a knowledge society.

At the same time, it must be ensured that cognitive and language skills, for which the Indian education system is recognised, is not diluted.

Vocational Education

Vocational education in India has unfortunately still not become socially acceptable. Academic courses have tended to ignore practical aspects. Vocational courses are perceived as courses meant for the less bright students.

Vocational training and skill development to inculcate a sense of pride in doing by one's own hands and to induce a respect for dignity of labour has to receive sufficient focus. Vocational training has to be compulsorily given in an intensive manner at the secondary level.

Distance Education

The potential for distance education in India has been largely untapped. World wide, there has been a strong component of technology in the spread of distance education. Distance education is cost effective, has reach and is a challenging process by itself. Distance education must be promoted not as a correspondence course, but as an alternative system of education on par with the formal system of education.

Value Systems

It is internationally accepted that education must inculcate values in children, leading them to be good citizens. Value education is the very definition of education. Unfortunately, training of young minds on values has taken a backseat in Indian society, given its obsession with material pursuits. Compounding this is the fact that there are hardly any role models in public life. Today there is a crisis of character in Indian society.

To build a society with good character and citizenship, it is important that value education is introduced in pre-school and reinforced in primary, secondary and higher education. At the same time, there have to be safeguards against advertent or inadvertent creeping in of various 'isms'.

Common National Content

A centralised system for curriculum, examinations and funding has brought about gross inadequacies in the learning process, infrastructure, facilities, effectiveness of expenditure and innovation at the institutional level.

As of now there are different boards of studies for primary and secondary school education. The State Boards, the Central Board of Secondary Education and the Indian Certificate for Secondary Education have varying content, standards and acceptance.

A common national system for educational content at the school level is necessary to bring about better standards. At the same time, there must be provision to accommodate regional and local variations and perspectives, especially with respect to languages, history and culture.

However, at the college, institution and university levels, the endeavour has to be to encourage innovation and creativity in content and process, within a broadly defined national framework.

A common national system looks difficult in the context of education being in the concurrent list of the Constitution. However, the challenge is worth taking in the interest of the future of our younger generation.

Decentralisation of Management

Education management, on the contrary, must be decentralised. Financing and management of education at the primary and secondary level as well as literacy programmes must devolve down to Panchayat levels. Panchayats must be encouraged to seek funding from the local community to supplement state funding. Central and state assistance should not be seen as largesse but linked to those who can help themselves. There are, of course, exceptions in the form of poor and backward areas. Decentralised management can help bring about better accountability, better utilisation of resources and greater people participation in the future of their children.

Common Admission Tests

Students seeking admission to higher education and professional courses are required to undergo a number of examinations in order to qualify. This is simply an utter callousness of the existing system and is largely wasteful.

A common system for admissions to professional courses needs to be instituted based on national level standardised tests on the lines of SAT, GRE and GMAT. Students can write these tests as many times as they want, and the best score would be considered. Each test score would have a validity of three years. These test scores would form the basis for admission purposes.

Concurrently, the system of migration certificates should be abolished and students should be free to move from one institution to another based on a system of transfer of professional credits.

Market Oriented Education

An important objective of education is to enhance one's standing in society and create economic value. The simplest measurement is the earning potential of the graduating student. The Indian education system is not market oriented. The failure of the system to realise the potential of the information technology requirements has led to a large non-formal education system of creating quality software professionals. These private institutions enjoy brand equity and large market capitalisation. The formal education system is not awake to the needs of society. Hence non-formal systems fill the need.

Schools of learning must be encouraged to constantly upgrade content and facilities in order to make them more market oriented. An independent rating system would also need to factor market valuation of products from schools of learning. At the same time, one must recognise that the market may not support education in such areas as oriental languages, archaeology, palaeontology, religion and philosophy. These educational programmes are important and necessary. It is here that the state will have to play an active role and support the pursuit of disciplines whose scholars do not command a market.

Education Infrastructure - Hardware

Just as economic infrastructure is seen as critical to an industrial society, the development of educational infrastructure must be seen as critical to a knowledge society. Infrastructure for schools - buildings, telecom networks, and computers - have to be funded on a priority basis. The government can progressively reduce the funding for universities to achieve this. These universities should take the path of self-sufficiency through higher students' fees, donations and endowments, alumni contributions, linkages with corporate establishments for research, royalties on books and research output etc. Thus UGC's role as a funding entity will no longer exist except to those areas of education involving liberal arts and performing arts.

Education Infrastructure - Content Development

Curricula in Indian schools of learning seldom reflect changing trends in the world. Periodic reviews undertaken show a lack of progressive thinking. A conservative approach is employed in development of curriculum. The result is that the students are ill prepared for the real world and require training on the job.

The stress should be on content development that will reflect latest advances in the subject. The Internet revolution has made it possible for information to be disseminated in real-time. This needs to be fully utilised to develop content that will be contemporary. This would involve fully utilising the ERNET and if necessary, expanding its reach.

Higher education should incorporate courses in the emerging technologies in areas such as telecommunication, robotics, automation and biotechnology and constantly seek to embrace new and emerging disciplines. In the traditional courses, the focus should be on cutting edge technologies and courses. For instance, in Civil Engineering the cutting edge technology would involve constructing intelligent buildings and intelligent roads.

Government Role

Given sustained large fiscal deficits of the Government of India and state Governments, the outlays on social sectors have been low. Most of the outlays are spent on salaries and wages. Given this situation, the tax payer's money is better spent on improving literacy, primary education, secondary education and education that is not market oriented while private sector money needs to be attracted for institutions of higher learning.

The responsibility of the Government must be confined only to funding and ensuring that primary education is compulsory and free, funding and ensuring that secondary education is compulsory, funding and bringing about 100% literacy, supporting disciplines that have no market orientation, selectively supporting and part funding centres of higher learning, providing financial guarantees for student loans, ensuring uniformity in content and quality, and planning.

In succeeding levels of education, the Government should play the role of a facilitator. Government must exercise its regulatory role to streamline higher education to ensure that it is meaningful, purposeful and cost effective. In essence, the Government's role should be maximum at the primary stage and minimum at the higher education stage.

Government Controls

The education sector in India is probably the most controlled sector in India. The whole mindset is on grants and aids. Arising out of this mindset is a plethora of rules and regulations. There are far too many bodies managing education. Rules and regulations govern virtually everything from location, student intake, course content, fees and fee structure, appointments, compensation for faculty and so on.

This is the equivalent of government imposing controls on an industrial unit's location, capacity, raw material intake, technology, compensation package, product prices, recruitment etc. on the back of subsidies and grants.

Consequently, institutions of learning have become rigid. There is little freedom for creativity and innovation. The compensation system is unable to attract good quality faculty. Research initiatives are constrained and linkages with private sector are poor.

The whole system needs to be overhauled. Institutions that do not depend on the government for funding or have low levels of funding must have operational freedom and the flexibility to innovate. Management of education must be decentralised.

Private Universities

A redefinition of government role in higher education would call for a major privatisation of the university education system in India. A Private University bill should be legislated to encourage establishment of new private universities in the fields of science and technology, management, economics, financial management and other critical areas with commercial application.

These new private universities should offer courses in emerging areas of science and technology and respective areas. They must be encouraged to aim for world class standards that would revolve around research based learning, an open environment, people based competencies, best in class facilities, market oriented curriculum, attractive performance based compensation packages and an unfailing accent on quality.

Business and industry have a vital role to play in establishing world class institutes of higher learning. Leading business houses must be encouraged to establish such institutes and universities.

Rating System

The quality of education imparted in India is diverse. For example, in technical education the quality ranges from the globally recognised Indian Institutes of Technology to fly-by-night engineering colleges. Educational institutions in India are neither rated nor benchmarked. There is no demand on teachers to constantly upgrade skills. While institutions exhort students to be competitive, they themselves have no motivation to be competitive as schools of learning. The employment market has created a non-formal assessment of institutions but there is no formal system in place.

There are anomalies as well. The University Grants Commission is responsible for quality of universities. However the Indira Gandhi National Open University and the All India Council of Technical Education are outside its purview. All educational institutions in India - schools, colleges, institutions and universities- must be rated by independent agencies analogous to a Standard and Poor's or CRISIL in the financial sector. There should be an annual review by the rating agency.

Rating should mandatorily cover some important issues such as emphasis on girls' education, value education, social service, physical education and games. This rating should be mentioned in the prospectus as well as all important communications. Initially, higher educational institutions should comply with rating requirements. After a defined period of time, the rating system should be extended to schools as well.

Funding to educational institutions must be linked to rating. Institutions with a lower than the minimum specified rating should not be allowed to operate. An independent rating system will bring about accountability in the education system in India. It will motivate schools of learning to be performance oriented and competitive. It will push teachers and faculty to be contemporary. Based on ratings, a differential fee structure could emerge. On the whole, a system that continuously seeks higher standards of performance would emerge. This is important for

Indian society to progress in a far more intensively competitive world.

Foreign Direct Investment

Almost all sectors in India, save such sectors as defence, atomic energy and education, are open to foreign direct investment. In the education sector, such investments are cleared on a case to case basis and there are very few instances. Foreign direct investment in education will have the benefit of improving standards and quality of education. It can facilitate global integration of the Indian education which, even to date, is not accepted in many professional disciplines such as medicine and accounting.

The Government should allow foreign direct investment in education. To begin with, this can be limited to education in science and technology. In other areas, there could be a possibility of external cultural influences coming in through foreign direct investment and hence may not be allowed.

Financing

The massive investment in education involved in creating a knowledge society needs to be financed. An education development fund needs to be set up for primary and literacy education. Donations to this fund to be fully exempt for income tax purposes.

The Government of India should utilise this fund for primary and secondary education, development of disciplines that the market cannot support, higher education on a selective basis and for creating the required infrastructure for education.

Privatisation of higher and professional education can relieve government funding from these areas which can be used for primary education and improving literacy. Subsidies for higher education should be gradually withdrawn through higher fees and changes in fee structure.

Concurrently, a credit market for education needs to be developed to support financing the higher costs. Financial institutions should be encouraged to offer assistance in the form of loans to students in higher education and professional streams. Introducing loans improves resource allocation since students will enrol in courses with better returns. It will also attract resources to the education sector as it is linked to graduates' future earnings. Since sufficient collateral cannot be provided by students, a scheme for government guarantees coupled with an independent recovery authority needs to be institutionalised.

Marketing Indian Education Abroad

India is currently being seen by foreign universities from UK, USA, Canada and Australia as a huge market for their educational services. The quality of educational services rendered by some of these universities is questionable, but such concerns get clouded in our society's blind charm for foreign labels and degrees.

This process has to be reversed. Indian institutions and universities must be able to attract overseas students. There is a good market for Indian education in Asia, Africa, South America and East Europe. Our cost levels will easily be less than one fourth of those in the developed world with comparable quality.

The Indian education system, once reformed, will have the ability to attract a large number of foreign students. This will have to be encouraged in order to generate additional finances and earn goodwill. To begin with the establishment of international schools in all our existing centres of excellence, which have international reputation, can be started.

Politicisation

Our universities have become hot beds of politics. The teacher turned politicians in universities are largely responsible for falling standards and commitment. University unions are seen as nurseries for political careers. To remedy this serious malady it is important that all political parties come to an understanding that they will keep away from universities and educational institutions. This may seem to be an utopian idea. However a beginning in this direction is overdue. It is also important to bring about legislation banning any form of political activity on campuses of universities and educational institutions.

Education and Economic Freedom

Education is not the only input for creating a knowledge based society. Economic opportunities are equally important. Education is necessary but not enough. Opportunities to harness education and knowledge need to be created. This would necessitate an economy free from controls that fosters new opportunities. These new opportunities, in turn, place new demands on education. They also help reverse the process of brain drain. In this sense, reforms in education and in the economy are mutually reinforcing.

Research in Education

Research in India is largely an elitist concept. Research at all levels starting from the Undergraduate level in the science and technology fields should be encouraged. Even the infrastructure available for research and development is poor and archaic.

The industrial growth is estimated to be around 12 to 15 % in the coming years. This would mean not only a large requirement of trained graduates but also providing continuing education for upgrading the skill and knowledge of technical personnel working in industry and service sectors. There are meagre efforts to address this large segment. This could be a potential money-spinner for the educational institution. Universities and institutions should establish separate administrative department to focus on this segment. The faculty should be drawn from those teaching the regular classes. The faculty will also benefit from interaction with the industry personnel.

Physical Education

There is no emphasis on physical development in our school curriculum. There is a need to encourage sports activities by providing the necessary infrastructure. The existing resources of Sports Authority of India and other sports bodies in the country should be utilised for this critical area.

Extra-curricular Activities

One day per week (preferably Saturday) has to be compulsorily set aside for extra-curricular activities such as games, study trips, arts and crafts and similar activities at the primary school and secondary school level.

Upgrading RECs and ITIs

The Regional Engineering Colleges can be upgraded by allowing them more autonomy to raise additional resources for upgradation of their resources. This has to be taken up on priority to ensure that the quality of RECs are comparable to the existing IITs.

Industrial Training Institutes (ITI) established in the late sixties provided a large number of skilled and semi-skilled manpower for both Indian and Persian Gulf companies. However, over the years, they have gradually lost their position due to non-upgradation of their curriculum and infrastructure. India's growth aspirations would need a large number of skilled manpower and these ITI can meet these requirements. Urgent steps should be taken to upgrade the infrastructure, resources and curriculum of these ITI s.

2

ASPIRATIONS OF INDIAN SOCIETY

MAKING EDUCATION IN INFORMATION AGE

Telecommunication via geostationary satellites and the worldwide network of computers have made the world a global village. Real time electronic communication between any two computers connected to the network, irrespective of their spatial separation, can be realised using the Internet. This is possible because the electromagnetic signals move in the network with the speed of light. Unlike the cost of travel, which is directly related to the physical distance between the starting point and the destination, the cost of electronic communication is independent of it. The Internet has thus shrunk the world in both space and time and made the concept of national frontiers as notional as the boundary lines drawn on a globe.

In a village, the education of children in addition to being the prerogative of the parents is a community responsibility, because children grow up together. Likewise in the present context, education of children who now live in a global village may have to be viewed with a broader perspective than as isolated national concerns. Only with a regional perspective of education that cuts across language barriers and cultural diversities it may become possible for us to enable our children to grow up together. This will require that our children study in a global classroom. As already mentioned Internet offers the possibility to realise teaching and learning in a " global classroom."

India being a vast country is full of diversity not only in its social and cultural structure but also in its educational system. There are 32 States and Union Territories in India. It is therefore not surprising that the structure of education in the country became extremely heterogeneous as it evolved in the States in response to aspirations and contextual needs of the regional population. Therefore, the most important task for the Central and the State governments, which work together in a federal set up, was to adopt a common structure of education. Several Commissions on Education, at different times in the fifty years since independence, examined issues on education to meet the emerging needs of its people. That students throughout the country should attain comparable knowledge and competencies was accepted as an important challenge for the educational system.

Because of recent efforts, the country has finally adopted a uniform structure of education. The structure has been split into three stages, comprising 10 + 2 +3 years of studies. Of these the first twelve years form the school education and the next three years leading to first degree form the higher education. The first ten years of school education are used for transacting an undifferentiated general education curriculum. The next two years form the higher secondary stage. It provides diversification into academic and vocational streams and is preparatory to professional and tertiary education. The assessment of performance of students is carried out by each school for its students, except for two public examinations, conducted by as many as 34 Boards of School Education, at the end of the 10th and the 12th year of school studies.

The varying standards of assessment of performance by the different Boards of School Education are a nightmare to students, who have to compete for admission to national institutions by writing common entrance tests, though they would have studied in schools with varying learning conditions and with different curricula. In 1993, the total enrolment of students studying in classes I to XII was 154,223,500 and, of these, those who were studying in classes XI-XII alone were 7,170,766. The total number of seats for professional education in the country is less than 100,000. Admission to professional courses is either based on performance in public examinations or in entrance tests or in their combination. Because of clamour for obtaining admission to professional courses, students tune their learning to the pattern of tests of the Boards and those of the entrance tests.

The pressure to perform well in public examinations and entrance tests results in a " backwash effect ". Only what is tested is taught and learnt! In reality, the prevailing practice is that some selected course contents are hand picked for testing. Learning becomes bookish and is reduced to mastering of clever tricks for performing well in these tests. Moreover, as the public examinations are administered to a vast number of students, they are impersonal and cannot assess individual skills. When students are asked whether the 10 years of general education or the additional 2 years of higher secondary education have given them the skills required for their viability in the society, the common answer is " NO." When the situation has reached such an impasse, the way out may have to be found not in tinkering of the existing system but by providing a radical change to it.

The changing nature of work and the global emergence of an information age provide the context for determining the change. Today, the world has changed. More and more jobs have become skilled. The youth will have to possess the skills required for initial employment and the ability to learn new skills to keep pace with the changing nature of work. Another dimension to consider is that employment opportunities will be preferentially available to those who possess the required skills irrespective of their nationality. Therefore, young persons will require an education that can provide them better appreciation of life and culture in societies other than that of the society in which they grow up. The other crucial factor is the influence of information technology in nearly all occupations.

Each person will have to learn how to use the computer as a tool in the work that he/she may be doing and have the generic skills for using information technology effectively. Some of these skills are problem solving, critical thinking, decision making, accessing information, processing and dissemination of information after providing value addition to it. In the context of these concerns, we at the National Council of Educational Research and Training (NCERT) have planned a programme for using computer as a resource in schools. Broadly, it comprises of development of competencies for using computer in stand-alone mode, in network and for learning by using both offline and online educational resources. The online learning by a student can be the use of e-mail in carrying out collaborative projects of mutual interest with some other student elsewhere in the world, accessing of information of interest form the world wide web with the help of search engines and using it in her project. Because of the high cost of hardware and software, and the limitation of accessibility to Intenet, it is proposed to try a pilot experiment first.

Bringing Learners Together

The project aims at giving advantage of the vast educational resources available in the countries of the region, elsewhere in the world and those of the NCERT to students and their teachers through the Internet and other communication technologies. The personality of a child is shaped in a cultural context. By enabling young persons to grow up together in an interactive environment with peers in different countries will help them to attain comparable intellectual heights and develop international understanding. To make this happen we require participation of appropriate organisations in the region for working with us on the project. It may be pointed out that schools in India emphasise mastery of discrete units of fixed knowledge through teaching of traditional school subjects such as languages, mathematics, science and social sciences.

What is required is that though learning may continue to be around traditional subjects, the learning experiences may be reoriented for developing learning to learn, decision making skills, communication skills and interpersonal skills. These can be achieved by exposing students to real life problems, involving for their solution a collaborative effort. Implementation of such an approach will require that schools, irrespective of their physical separation, arrange for their students to interact with one another to enable them to work on problems that can be best solved collectively. The Internet provides an effective mode for enabling interaction in spite of physical separation. In addition, the global networking of computers has made it possible to share educational resources without encumbrance and that too at near zero cost.

Individuals and institutions are putting up information on every conceivable area of human interest on the Internet. Information on education, especially school education such as lesson plans, test items and supplementary instructional materials on a wide spectrum of school subjects are available on the Internet in an organised and easy-to-access form. The Internet is an ideal medium for interactive self-learning and if used intelligently will develop learning to learn. Therefore, the computer and the network to which it may be connected have to be used as tools for achieving the stated objectives and not as subjects of study. In order to provide such a learning environment to a group of children in India the following steps would be taken:

1. Selection of a cluster of State-run schools in New Delhi and Bangalore (in view of availability of access to the Internet and expert support in these cities) for taking part in the project (as global communication will be crucial to the project, these schools should have sections of students who use English as the medium of study),

2. Involvement of children in the age group 13-16 in the project,
3. Association of local experts to provide support to the participating schools and in the monitoring of the programme.

The following assessable competencies will be developed through appropriate activities. Each student should be able to

— boot the system, run a programme, use help and tutorials, open a file, save a file, locate a file, copy a file, print a file, etc.,

— work in the Win 95 or Win NT environment,

— use with facility MS Office for word processing, database management and spreadsheet,

— generate tables and charts,

— create graphic objects using graphic tools,

— plan layout of documents and prepare them in aesthetically appealing form for desk top publishing by insertion of images, tables, charts and graphic objects in text,

— scan images using a scanner,

— send and receive electronic-mail,

— attach files with e-mail and to open attachments received with e-mail,

— send and receive FAX using computer,

— log on to the Internet,

— open a web site from its URL,

— find information using search engines, select and classify information from the search findings,

— use hyperlinks for surfing on the Net,

— save selected information from web sites into folders and make their hard copy by using a printer,

— work on collaborative projects with peers using e-mail.

It is expected that these competencies will make students information technology literate and at the same time will develop in them the confidence to upgrade their skills, as they would have acquired the ability of learning to learn. The competency XVI is what we want to realise through a collaborative venture. In the following paragraphs, we have visualised a programme in which students from India will be able to assist international students to understand India better. We expect that similar approach would be reciprocated by collaborating organisations in helping international students in general and students from India in particular to understand their country better.

The topics on which the Indian students should be able to carry out in-depth study and acquire information that they can share over the Internet with their international peers, say students in Australia, are those that they have inherited, grown up with or have easy access to. For them, it would be a voyage into their own heritage and culture for discovering India. If similar approach is adopted by all the participating countries the children with their knowledge, understanding and experience will be able to mutually benefit and develop a realistic appreciation of each other's culture.

Role of NCERT

The NCERT is an apex organisation in India, which through its programmes such as curriculum development, publication of textbooks, teacher education, educational technology, vocational education, research and extension provides resource support to school education in the country. We have recently set up a computer resource centre at the NCERT headquarters in New Delhi. As the principal resource centre on school education in India, the NCERT would co-ordinate this project and collaborate with its counterparts in other participating countries.

Other responsibilities of the NCERT would be:

— Development of modules for students for acquiring the planned competencies

— Training of teachers

— Networking with professionals for providing expert support

— Obtaining feedback from students

— Making available on the Internet its resources

— Answering students queries by e-mail

It is accepted that a majority of schools in India have inadequate infrastructure and it may not be possible for the State to provide computers in sufficient numbers to each school for implementing the above programme. If with the pilot project, it can be convincingly shown that children who are information technology literates have an edge in an information society, the community may come forward to meet the needed support.

ASPIRATION VERSUS REALITY

The Indian software industry has compiled an impressive track record over the past decade. Entrepreneurs, bureaucrats and politicians are now advancing views about how India can transform itself into a knowledge-based economy by riding the information technology (IT) bandwagon. Isolated instances of villagers using e-mail are cited as examples of such transformation. Likewise, e-governance is being projected as the way of the future. At a computer training centre in Kozhikode, Kerala. India's real progress into a knowledge economy will not come without a substantial development of its human potential.

There is no dearth of fascinating stories about IT-enabled changes. But, there is little discussion about whether such changes are sustainable and effective when other areas of the economy continue to lag. For example, 79 per cent of India's population lives in villages with limited basic infrastructure. Over 60 per cent of the population is considered literate, but with literacy being defined as the ability to read and write simple words in any language, acquired with or without formal schooling. This criterion is so basic, that it is almost irrelevant in the context of a knowledge economy. Yet, Central and State governments have projected IT as a vehicle for social and economic transformation. Are we putting the cart before the horse here? Even if the focus on IT is justifiable, how must IT policy be designed so that the nation is benefited in a balanced way?

India should aggressively pursue manufacturing- and agriculture-based industries to build a robust industrial economy that can be made more efficient with IT. IT projects can certainly be pursued within the private sector. However, government policy should not be heavily skewed in favour of the IT industry when its benefits to society are unclear and when its role within the broader framework of national development has not been adequately articulated. Further, policy-makers should moderate their obsession with IT as a panacea for India's socio-economic problems.

Booms and busts have long existed in various markets. For example, during the tulip bubble in 1637, the irrational exuberance of buyers drove up the value of each tulip to several thousand dollars. A single Semper Augustus tulip was then three times as valuable as the most expensive estate in Amsterdam. However, apart from such frivolous booms and busts, even serious researchers (including Stephen Roach, the Chief Economist at Morgan Stanley) have struggled to demonstrate convincingly the benefits of IT. This reflects the widely recognised IT "productivity paradox". Equally important, proponents of the "new growth theory", including noted Stanford University economist Paul Romer, have convincingly argued that human capital, which is a function of education levels and workforce skills, is a crucial input for economic growth.

Human capital generates the ideas and knowledge that, in turn, decide how efficiently and effectively the traditional inputs of capital (such as plant and equipment) and labour are translated into output. The message is that an enormous pool of labour, in itself, is of limited value. Real progress into a knowledge economy will not come without a substantial development of India's human potential. Against this backdrop, Indian policy planners and politicians must ponder the following issues. The value of IT depends greatly on the existing level of economic development.

IT can make existing assets and processes more effective and efficient, but cannot compensate for the lack of a basic infrastructure. What is appropriate for a developed economy is not necessarily appropriate for India, where basic elements of infrastructure including quality education, healthcare, electricity and drinking water remain in short supply. The impact of IT is best understood when the differences between industrial and knowledge-intensive ventures are recognised. Industrial growth derives from investments in large-scale infrastructure (such as railways, roadways, power grids and dams).

Such infrastructure supports the growth of physical-asset intensive industries (such as the steel and transportation industries) that create and move physical entities (such as goods, water and people). These ventures employ numerous workers with limited education and skills, and can uplift large sections of society. In contrast, ventures in the knowledge economy usually involve the production of knowledge-intensive goods (like software), and the large-scale capture, movement and utilisation of information using sophisticated network infrastructure (such as computers, cable, fibre and routers). Beyond the physical labour required for initial construction, building and maintaining such infrastructure requires specialised knowledge.

Despite the hype of the "new economy", the fact is that economic development is cumulative. The industrial economy made agriculture more productive. The productivity of agricultural labour skyrocketed with the use of industrial and biological innovations including tractors, irrigation systems, fertilizers, pesticides and genetically engineered seeds. Historically, industrial innovation in developed economies has created great wealth and improved living standards across societal divides. This progress has set them up in an ideal position to create and exploit knowledge as they transform into knowledge-based economies.

Crucially, the greatest source of productivity and growth attributed to the knowledge economy derives not from the knowledge economy itself, but from its effects on the industrial economy. For example, IT can enable supply chains and factories to work more efficiently. The "leapfrogging" argument, whereby India skips heavy infrastructure building and transforms directly into a knowledge economy, is therefore suspect. Proponents of leapfrogging describe how isolated villages without conventional telephones have directly adopted cellular phones. The example provides excellent symbolism. However, the underlying principle is not scalable to the level of the national economy where many complex sub-systems work together. Consider the transportation sub-system.

The laws of physics do not allow IT to substitute the physical movement of goods by a "virtual" movement. A lightning-fast information network will not in itself help achieve faster and cheaper transport. Better roadways and railways will.

IT, job growth and government policy

INDIAN IT firms have focussed on developing and delivering IT services to advanced economies. Even if India became the world's software factory and the most optimistic projections of IT-related jobs (including jobs in call centres and design centres) were upheld, this industry will employ at most a few million people. In a nation with over a billion people, this constitutes but a dent in the employment statistics. Further, a social planner should be concerned not just with the creation of wealth, but also with its distribution across social divides. The IT industry holds limited potential for wealth to trickle down to the poorer sections of society. Unlike a steel plant, IT engenders few opportunities for the uneducated.

Any transfer of wealth from the IT sector (for example, by taxing the IT sector to fund social spending) would be achieved through the heavy hand of government. This represents, at best, a dubious economic proposition. In fact, the rapid growth of IT will likely lead to a digital divide in the short term, where the rich and educated are empowered and enriched by IT and the poor are oblivious to its impact. Before embracing IT, Indian policy planners must carefully evaluate whether investments in other areas would yield higher, and more equitable, returns. For example, consider the jute industry. This industry sustains over five million Indian households.

In the late 1980s, while working for an industrial development bank, one of us was puzzled by the government's blanket ban on the use of plastic (for example, high density poly ethylene) to package cement, fertilizers, foodgrains and other commodities - only jute was to be used. Considering that jute bags were more prone to spillage and rat-induced destruction, this regulation appeared to have no rational economic basis. (Jute packaging has improved much since then.) However, this policy had some important redeeming features when viewed from a social perspective. But, can India employ technology in the jute industry to achieve both economic and social objectives?

Imagine using the power of technology (including IT) to derive new and innovative uses for jute; to expand the domestic and export market base for jute products; to position jute as a natural, inexpensive and biodegradable substitute for plastics; and to improve the efficiency of local jute markets so that jute growers can get better prices. Now imagine how these initiatives could benefit millions of Indian households. This does not call for every jute cultivator to access the Internet. A public or private agency with the right incentives and with access to domestic and international marketplaces can orchestrate these initiatives. Governmental incentives for research and development (R&D) related to improving jute products and finding new uses for jute would deliver more benefits to jute farmers, than would e-mail access.

As illustrated in the case of the jute industry, Indian policy planners frequently overlook two important points. First, the creative application of IT in a range of manufacturing and agricultural industries can yield much greater returns at a societal level, compared with software production and export. Second, not all technology is information technology - traditional R&D related to design and manufacturing remains extremely important. Such R&D can be enhanced by IT (for example, via virtual collaboration and computer aided design), but not substituted by it.

The country needs to be particularly careful not to give short shrift to the manufacturing sector. China is not known for its strengths in IT, although it now has some presence in the area. But, what China has accomplished in terms of its core industrial base is striking. Foreign direct investment (FDI) in China was of the order of $40 billion in 2000 despite all the noise about alleged labour and human rights abuses. Chinese exports exceeded $200 billion in 2000, with the United States alone accounting for $100 billion of these exports. In fact, the value of "footwear" exported annually by China to the U.S. (worth about $9.2 billion) itself compares with or even exceeds the total value of India's annual IT exports.

Why are these numbers relevant? Exporting footwear creates millions of jobs for citizens who lack sophisticated skills. According to some reports, a total of 34 million export-related jobs have been created in China, with exports to the U.S. alone accounting for over 20 million jobs in the last decade. These jobs have improved living standards for a substantial fraction of Chinese society. There is much we need to learn from China about how the manufacturing sector can deliver robust and equitable economic growth. Taiwan, Malaysia and South Korea have also flourished using similar approaches. In contrast with manufacturing, the direct benefits to IT (such as employment in IT jobs) are likely to flow to the few who already have the benefits of education.

The trickle-down effects of IT (such as cleaning and maintenance staff for IT firms) are likely to be modest or non-existent outside the large cities. The benefits of IT implementation across other industrial sectors (such as employing IT to make transportation and supply chains more efficient) will likely be substantial, but Indian industrial policy does not point in this direction at the moment. It is also time to discard the notion that the manufacturing sector is inherently less appealing because it may involve some physical labour. In the more advanced economies, a skilled factory floor worker is frequently paid more than a call-centre employee. Empowered with technology, the factory worker can add value at a remarkable rate. In India, the reverse often holds.

Mundane call-centre jobs, often outsourced from more developed economies, absorb well-educated, English-speaking workers whose abilities could be employed much more productively elsewhere. The emphasis on IT would be less objectionable if it did not contrast sharply with the treatment meted out to other industrial sectors. Consider the Vijayanagar steel plant. The plant had the potential to transform the poverty-stricken Bellary district in Karnataka. The feasibility study for the plant was completed in 1967 and its foundation was laid in 1972. Finally, in 1995, more than a quarter century later, the government divested its interests in the (yet incomplete) project.

A scaled-down, modified version of the project is now up and running under the auspices of the private sector. Meanwhile, the market for steel has evolved to an extent that the assumptions that anchored the initial feasibility study are worthless. The actions of governments in India tend to be biased in favour of the IT sector. For instance, software taxes levied in Karnataka were removed within a week in response to pressure from IT companies. Many workplace inspection procedures have been suspended for IT companies, while other sectors are subjected to myriad regulations, many of which have not been re-evaluated for relevance and effectiveness for decades. The government needs a more balanced policy, one that ensures that the core industrial sector is not ignored in the rush toward IT.

IT and education

IT is fashionable to say that India's population constitutes its greatest asset. This viewpoint is misleading. People are assets only when they participate meaningfully in the cycle of value creation and consumption by exercising buying power, or creating products and services of value, or by creating and harnessing knowledge. A large fraction of India's population does not meet, or even come close to, this asset standard. To transform such a situation, a renewed focus is required on the two pillars that have supported the growth of every successful economy - a strong infrastructure core and widespread access to education. Now to discuss the IT-education interface.

Distance learning and e-learning are already being flaunted in some quarters as solutions to India's education challenges. The argument proffered is that IT can enable the cheap and widespread delivery of education. This reasoning ignores the key challenge - how can the children of the poor and the uneducated be provided with the incentives to come to school, stay in school, and progress to higher institutions of learning? The answer lies in understanding physiology, psychology and economics, rather than in implementing technology. For all its drawbacks and implementation problems, the mid-day meal programme launched by the late Chief Minister M.G. Ramachandran in Tamil Nadu addressed this challenge head on.

The programme recognised a simple, but fundamental, fact the brain cannot feed when the stomach itself is unfed. It provided parents with the incentive to send their children to schools, rather than to the fields. For the children to whom the benefits of education seemed like a distant, hazy mirage, it provided an immediate, tangible reason to stay in school. There is little reason to believe that IT-based learning will advance meaningfully the cause of Indian education. Problems that are enmeshed in the social and economic fabric of Indian society need to be addressed primarily with solutions that are of a social and economic nature. Throwing technology at these problems will not make them go away. In addition, creating the infrastructure and content to support effective e-learning is very expensive.

Many universities in the U.S. are still struggling to achieve effectively learning objectives in the virtual setting. This problem will be compounded in the Indian environment owing to the diversity of languages and the lack of infrastructure. A rush into e-learning at this stage will only lead to squandered resources. Presenting technology as the solution to India's educational challenges is troublesome in two ways. First, it diverts attention from issues that should really be on the front-burner. Once this happens, building back momentum in the correct direction is difficult. Second, by building castles in the air that will soon be blown away by the winds of reality, it does a serious disservice to the more limited, but yet substantial and real benefits of technology.

IT and Culture

A knowledge economy is characterised by a culture of innovation. For such a culture to take root, innovation must be rewarded and intellectual property must be protected. A culture that truly enhances innovation supports the view that to try hard and fail is perfectly fine. Yet, the Indian psyche has historically been averse to blessing the risky venture. In fact, education has been viewed as a way to avoid risky options, rather than as an enabler of intelligent risk-taking and entrepreneurship. Such a cultural mindset hinders innovation because meaningful innovation is almost never without significant risk.

This attitude transcends into the corporate arena. Consider how static the Indian automobile industry was for three decades before the refreshing winds of competition brought about rapid change. Competition breeds innovation. Not surprisingly, even as markets have become increasingly competitive, R&D spending by U.S. firms has increased sharply, at an annual rate of over 6 per cent during the period 1995-2000. While one side of the cultural coin pertains to the incentives for innovation, the flip side pertains to its protection. Ideas, unlike property, cannot be protected by building a fence around them. Intellectual property protection is not a purely economic issue; it also has important cultural dimensions.

The economic angle can be addressed with stronger patent laws and punitive procedures. However, the cultural angle will decide whether such protection can be enforced meaningfully. Addressing the cultural angle is a challenge. It requires that even without the threat of punishment, one should learn to draw a clear, disciplined boundary in everyday life between what is one's to take and keep, and what is not. Making such a cultural shift requires that India stop treating intellectual property rights in a casual manner. For example, a frequent argument heard in support of piracy goes along these lines - "If we could afford it, we would pay for it. We pirate because we cannot pay for it." But then, how does an inability to pay for something ever translate into a justification to obtain it for free? One would be highly challenged to apply this logic to hotel stays, vacations, or even a television set. Piracy exists in every economy, but rampant piracy dilutes the incentive to innovate. In the context of intellectual property, economic measures and cultural shifts should proceed hand-in-hand before the spirit of Indian entrepreneurship can take full flight.

A society that is deeply divided by social and economic fissures must think carefully about how it achieves economic and technological advance. The path, in some ways, is more important than the outcome itself. The economic travails of modern-day Russia provide a striking example of the results of chaotic advance. In the Indian context, particular attention needs to be paid to when, where, and in what form IT and other technological advances are encouraged. There are, indeed, many low-hanging fruits to be harvested. For example, a recent article in The New York Times described how a fisherman working off the coasts of Kerala used a cellphone on the seas to obtain information about spot market prices for fish at Kochi and Kollam.

The fisherman netted the equivalent of an additional \$1,000 in annual income merely by deciding to deliver his catch to the more remunerative market each time his boat came in. This striking example of how simple information flows can enhance market efficiency can be replicated in many ways, and in many markets. However, the stakes are quite different when it comes to the formulation of a national IT policy. Any national policy requires some trade-offs between the benefits to industrial sectors, regions and classes of people.

In formulating a national IT policy, the quest for superior technology must be moderated by an understanding of its implications at the social level - what might be good for a private company or an entrepreneur may not always be good for society and vice-versa. For example, a municipal corporation that purchases automated road-laying equipment may find that it either does not use the equipment at all, or that it uses the equipment and allows numerous labourers on its payroll to idle. In this case, technology policy and labour policy are inextricably linked within the overall social context. It is shortsighted to advance doggedly on one front while turning a blind eye to the other.

Successful technology adoption will move in measured steps, at a pace and in a direction that are in harmony with changes in the socio-economic fabric. The role of the government in ensuring such harmony should not be underestimated. This is especially true in India where the government remains responsible for a significant fraction of the economic output, and where it is actively reshaping rules and regulations as the country integrates into the global economy. From the triumph of the capitalist systems across the globe, there is now ample empirical support for the view that governments must ultimately govern with a light touch. At the same time, several economies that have attempted rapid, unstructured transitions into the capitalist mode have declined. There is a strong argument to be made that the Indian government must not simply get out of the way in the spirit of laissez faire, but must instead play a key role in pacing and shaping this transition.

Information technology can change the way a society communicates, collaborates, lives, works and plays. The growth of the IT sector in India symbolises the potential of Indian industry to perform at world-class standards. This success demonstrates much of what can go right when the spirit of human enterprise is given free rein. However, the success of IT at the corporate level in India cannot solve its myriad economic and social challenges. Just as copious rainfall can lead to dramatic floods, an obsession with IT and the knowledge economy is not useful. To be truly beneficial, the rain of IT must fall at the right place in the right quantity, at the right time and for the right purpose.

Economic policies of a developing country cannot be based on "herd" behaviour and on what is hot in the international market for that year or decade. Neither does the aggressive pursuit of IT represent the sole, or even an obvious, pathway to a first class economy despite the glowing success of high-profile IT companies. Noted economist Paul Krugman, in arguing that someone who has made a personal fortune would not necessarily know how to make an entire nation more prosperous, phrased it best. "A country," he wrote in an article in the Harvard Business Review, "is not a company!"

3

Role and Functions

SOCIAL DEVELOPMENT

Education imparts knowledge and skills and shapes values and attitudes. It is vital for population control, poverty reduction, economic growth, civic order, culture and citizenship. Education helps reduce poverty by increasing the productivity of the poor, reducing fertility rates, improving health and equipping people with the skills they need to participate fully in the economy and in society. More generally, education helps strengthen civil institutions, build national capacity and good governance. These are critical elements for progress of a civil society.

ECONOMIC GROWTH

Education contributes to economic growth, but by itself does not generate growth. Various empirical analyses estimate that education explains about twenty per cent of growth in a country. The single largest contributor to this growth is primary education.

Historically, investment in education was considered more of a social obligation rather than one that would give significant returns. However, more recently, evidence has been accumulating to demonstrate that countries with high levels of basic education, whether developed or developing, show better economic performance.

An analysis of 60 countries (basic data in Table 1) shows that there is a good correlation between the real per capita GDP of a country and its adult literacy rate. Also, that there is a better correlation between the real per capita GDP of a country and its first, second and third level gross enrolment ratio. (Table 2)

Table 1

Basic data relating to education pertaining to 60 countries

Country	Real per capita GDP	Adult literacy rate	Combined first-, second- and third-level gross enrolment ratio	Public education expenditure
	PPP$	%	%	% of GDP
Algeria	4,460	60.3	68.0	5.2
Angola	1,430	45.0	27.0	1.0
Argentina	10,300	96.5	79.0	3.5
Australia	20,210	99.0	100.0	5.6
Bangladesh	1,050	38.9	35.0	2.9
Belgium	22,750	99.0	100.0	3.2
Bhutan	1,467	44.2	12.0	1.0
Brazil	6,480	84.0	80.0	5.2
Burkina Faso	1,010	20.7	20.0	3.6
Burundi	630	44.6	23.0	3.2
Canada	22,480	99.0	99.0	7.0
Central African Republic	1,330	42.4	26.0	1.0
Chad	970	50.3	29.0	1.0
China	3,130	82.9	69.0	2.3
Denmark	23,690	99.0	89.0	8.2
Egypt	3,050	52.7	72.0	1.0

Ethiopia	510	35.4	24.0	4.0
France	22,030	99.0	92.0	6.1
Germany	21,260	99.0	88.0	4.8
Greece	12,769	96.6	79.0	3.0
Hong Kong	24,350	92.4	65.0	2.9
Hungary	7,200	99.0	74.0	4.7
India	1,670	53.5	55.0	3.4
Indonesia	3,490	85.0	64.0	1.4
Iran	5,817	73.3	72.0	1.0
Iraq	3,197	58.0	51.0	1.0
Italy	20,290	98.3	82.0	4.7
Japan	24,070	99.0	85.0	3.6
Korea	13,590	97.2	90.0	3.7
Malaysia	8,140	85.7	65.0	5.2
Mali	740	35.5	25.0	2.2
Mexico	8,370	90.0	70.0	4.9
Mozambique	740	40.5	25.0	1.0
Myanmar	1,199	83.6	55.0	1.2
Nepal	1,090	38.1	59.0	3.1
Nigeria	920	59.5	54.0	0.9
Norway	24,450	99.0	95.0	7.5
Pakistan	1,560	40.9	43.0	3.0
Philippines	3,520	94.6	82.0	2.2
Portugal	14,270	90.8	91.0	5.5
Russian Federation	4,370	99.0	77.0	4.1
Rwanda	660	63.0	43.0	1.8
Senegal	1,730	34.6	35.0	3.5
Sierra Leone	410	33.3	30.0	1.0
Singapore	28,460	91.4	73.0	3.0
South Africa	7,380	84.0	93.0	7.9

Spain	15,930	97.2	92.0	4.9
Sri Lanka	2,490	90.7	66.0	3.4
Sudan	1,560	53.3	34.0	1.0
Sweden	19,790	99.0	100.0	8.3
Tanzania	580	71.6	33.0	1.0
Thailand	6,690	94.7	59.0	4.1
Uganda	1,160	64.0	40.0	2.6
United Kingdom	20,730	99.0	100.0	5.4
United States	29,010	99.0	94.0	5.4
Uruguay	9,200	97.5	77.0	3.3
Venezuela	8,860	92.0	67.0	1.0
Vietnam	1,630	91.9	62.0	2.7
Yemen	810	42.5	49.0	6.1
Zambia	960	75.1	49.0	2.2

Source: World Development Indicators 1999, The World Bank

Table 2.
Correlation coefficients on educaiton data pertaining to 60 countries (inpercentage)

Particulars	Real per capita GDP	Adult literacy rate	Combined first-, second- and third-level gross enrolment ratio	Public education expenditure as % of GNP
Real per-capita GDP	100.00			
Adult literacy rate	71.78	100.00		
Combined first-, second-				

and third level gross enrolment ratio	77.03	86.91	100.00	
Public education expenditure as % of GNP	59.68	47.80	64.98	100.00

Source: Business Intelligence Unit, Chennai

South East Asian countries are not rich in natural resources. Fast developers in this region have invested heavily in education. Countries that achieved universal basic education first (Korea being a prime example) were also the first ones to experience substantial economic growth.

A World Bank study in 1993 studied eight South East Asian economies - Hong Kong, Indonesia, Japan, Korea, Malaysia, Taiwan, Singapore and Thailand - and found that the single largest contributor to economic growth was primary education. Primary school enrolment explained between 58 percent (Japan) and 87 percent (Thailand) of predicted growth. The analysis concludes that there is a strong correlation between high levels of education and economic growth.

Interestingly, in the wake of the financial crisis, South East Asian countries are shoring up their educational systems to make them even stronger. In Thailand, a constitutional overhaul is laying the foundation for a radical shake up. Indonesia has introduced an emergency scholarship system. Singapore has begun a campaign to teach innovative thinking. Malaysia is launching computerised smart schools. The accent of these countries is on a quantum leap on basic education and skill standards to regain labour force competitiveness, shift from rote learning to creative thinking, less state dominance of education and making education more responsive to local needs.

Investment in Education

Education is an excellent investment for society. In general, the social rates of return to investment in all levels of education exceed the long-term opportunity cost of capital. Rates of return to education are very high in low and middle-income countries. (Table 3). Rates of return in education are also better than rates of return in other sectors such as agriculture, industry and infrastructure. (Table 4). Since education is subsidised almost everywhere in the world, private returns to investment in education invariably exceed social rates of return.

Table 3.

Rates of return to investment in education by region and level of schooling (in percentage)

Region	Social			Private		
	Primary	Secondary	Higher	Primary	Secondary	Higher
Sub-Saharan Africa	24.3	18.2	11.2	41.3	26.6	27.8
Asia	19.9	13.3	11.7	39	18.9	19.9
Europe, Middle-East and North Africa	15.5	11.2	10.6	17.4	15.9	21.7
Latin America and the Caribbean	17.9	12.8	12.3	26.2	16.8	19.7
OECD countries	n.a.	10.2	8.7	n.a.	12.4	12.3

Source: Priorities and strategies for education - A World Bank review 1995

Table 4.
Rates of return to investments in different sectors of the economy (inpercentage)

Educational investments	1974 to 1982
Primary	20
Secondary	14
Higher	11
World Bank projects	1983-92
Agriculture	11
Industry	12
Infrastructure	16
All projects	15

Source: Priorities and strategies for education
- A World Bank review 1995

Human Capital

Education is universally recognised as an important investment in building human capital. Human capital affects growth in two ways. First, human capital levels act as a driver of technological innovation. Second, human capital stocks determine the speed of absorption of technology. It is now widely accepted that human capital, and not physical capital, holds the key to persistent high growth in per capita income. This is because people, unlike machines, can learn. Investments that increase people skills and productivity, yield not diminishing returns, but constant or increasing returns.

Market Economy

Market economies now prevail in countries accounting for over 80 % of the world's population. This is a huge increase from the 30% figure that prevailed a decade ago. (Table 5) Market based systems reward enterprise, risk taking, skill and agility, but offer less security and a constantly changing environment.

In such a context, education is vital since those who compete best have an enormous advantage in the fast paced world economy.

Table 5.

Countries which have moved to market-based economies

Country	Population 1996 (Millions)
Algeria	29
Armenia	4
Azerbaijan	8
Bangladesh	122
Belarus	10
Bulgaria	8
China	1215
Croatia	5
Czech Republic	10
Estonia	1
Georgia	5
Hungary	10
India	945
Kazakhstan	16
Kyrgyz Republic	5
Latvia	2
Lithuania	4
Macedonia FYR	2
Nigeria	115
Poland	39
Romania	23
Russian Federation	148
Slovak Republic.	5
Slovenia	2
Tajikistan	6

Turkmenistan	5
Ukraine	51
Uzbekistan	23
Yugoslavia	11
Total population of these countries	2829
World population	5754
Percent	49.17%

Source: World Bank

Globalisation of markets and the factors that drive them - especially knowledge - is reinforcing these impacts. Global capital constantly seeks and flows to more favourable opportunities, including well trained, productive and attractively priced labour forces in a market friendly and politically stable business environment. Education will be at the centre stage in creating such an environment.

Knowledge Economy

Education is becoming even more vital in the new world of information. Knowledge is rapidly replacing raw materials and labour as the most critical input for survival and success. Knowledge has become the new asset. More than half of the GDP in the major OECD countries is now knowledge based. About two thirds of the growth of world GDP is expected to come from technology-led businesses (Table 6). This necessitates that education and knowledge are at the centre stage of any development process.

The global labour market is increasingly integrated for the highly knowledgeable and skilled - corporate executives, scientists and technologists - offering high mobility and wages. However, the market for unskilled labour is highly restricted by national and state barriers.

Table 6.
Global growth of technology led business
(in USD Billion)

Sector	Year 2000	Year 2010
Aerospace	70	160
Pharmaceuticals	300	1,100
Geomatics	10	60
Advanced Materials	450	880
Computer equipment	189	630
Internet	843	1,300
Software	785	2,300
Telecom services	270	630
Telecom equipment	250	500
Robotics and Automation	5	10
Total	3,172	7,560
Increase		4388
World GDP	30,000	36,600
Increase		6,600
%	11	21
% increase in share		66

Source: Reliance Research

Weightless goods - with high knowledge content rather than material content - now accounts for some of the most dynamic sectors in several economies. The single largest export industry for the United States is neither aircraft nor automobiles, but entertainment. Education offers a fast track to knowledge based growth.

A knowledge-based economy is not restricted to mean computers and information technology. It is a society where knowledge transcends all economic and social activities.

The agriculture sector is in a particularly vulnerable situation in the post-quantitative rate regime that will be upon the country very shortly. India is far behind in yield and productivity of principal crops. Valid fears arise over the country's food security. The industrial sector too has not seen much improvement in technology, or productivity. It has been harshly exposed to global competition over the last eight years. The services sector has advanced only in parts, and much needs to be done in the banking and insurance sectors.

Moving towards a knowledge-based economy should necessarily have the objective of causing a fundamental upward shift in the competitiveness of these sectors. Greater reforms coupled with targeted investments in education will make a substantial contribution in achieving this objective.

TECHNOLOGY IN EDUCATION

Technology has a pivotal role to play in the future of education. At one level it is through better use of existing communication technologies. Television and radio broadcasts offer important advantages to institutions involved in distance education . Broadcasting raises public awareness of the distance education institution, its programmes and in securing acceptance by the community at large of this alternative means of providing access to higher education .

The programmes are also important in providing distance education institutions with the opportunity to demonstrate excellence in academic content and teaching quality. This helps secure acceptance by the academic community for this innovative approach to learning. An appraisal of communications-based teaching which does not take these and related advantages into account is likely to underestimate the role of broadcasting in distance education.

At another level is the spread of information technology for revolutionising content and delivery of education. The Internet is capturing people who have never been touched by education. It is expected to become the school and the university for the dot com generations. In the United Kingdom, British Telecom is designing the "classroom of the future". A range of "virtual universities" is putting the latest technology to innovative use.

Internet offers policy-makers additional alternatives for delivering education and training to learners of all ages. This technology can reduce costs, increase access and expand the range and quality of education and training options. It offers poorer nations the chance to catch up. In Egypt, a government-backed project is developing a "utopian school", where pupils take "the best courses from the best teachers from around the world".

An increasing number of countries are experimenting with various forms of new technologies to expand education and training options. This is because they are able to develop multimedia materials that reflect local values and culture, provide visual images of desired behaviours, collaborate across borders, and access information not previously available.

The world of the future will have much more education occurring outside of schools. It will draw on vastly more powerful technologies, like the two-way voice-activated, computer-assisted and self-paced learning. Such technologies will harness a much better understanding of how people learn and what they need to learn. Learners will be able to go beyond the classroom and obtain information in a variety of forms - text, data, sound, video - from all over the world, at any time of the day or night and at rapidly diminishing costs.

Cyber-age Education

Half of all spheres of human activity in the world have got wired into a connectivity that has transcended national frontiers, geographical boundaries and even cosmic contours. It is an age that has brought to one's doorstep promises and prospects for unimaginable change and progress. Significant implications of the cyber age in the context of the potential role of education would be the following:

— Knowledge will no longer be a static, finite mass bound by space and time. It will be perpetually self-multiplying and self-renewing in proportion to R & D investments.

— The velocity of knowledge transmission will be incredibly fast. Geographical barriers to access to knowledge will no longer be operative. Access, of course, will be influenced and determined by socio-cultural, politico-economic, and personal factors.

— Generation, transmission, storage, retrieval, renewal and application of knowledge will not only be very largely helped and driven by technology, but will also be enhanced by it, in particular by technologies of information, communication and education.

— The world, having now increasingly adopted a market driven economy, information will tend to be commodified, will command an economic value, and therefore, will tend to create social classes of "haves" and "have-nots".

— Formal education will tend to be more a life long continuum, and dispersed rather than a one-shot limited period-centralised activity in respect of contents, instruction, materials, human resource, evaluation, accreditation, certification, and management.

— A rush to blend cyber-age education into the traditional education process must not be at the cost of elementary education, cognitive learning, physical activity and overall development. It must be realised that cyber-age education presents an option that is layered on top of a traditional system with its benefits of co-operative learning.

FUNDING

Government spending on education is often inefficient and inequitable. It is inefficient when it is misallocated among uses; it is inequitable when qualified potential students are unable to enrol in institutions because educational opportunities are lacking or because of their inability to pay.

A study of some developing countries in Africa and Middle East show that the Governments reallocate public spending to education from other publicly funded activities, such as defence and divestment of public enterprises. Other countries have, within their macroeconomic policies, increased the revenues of government and thereby increased the spend on education. Yet others have sought to supplement government funds for education with private funds.

Private financing can be encouraged either to fund private institutions or to supplement the income of publicly funded institutions. Private schools are usually financed through fees. In countries, which excessively regulate private schools, it is found that such restrictions discourage private spending on education that would otherwise have occurred and so increase the pressure on government funded schools. Another argument in favour of private schools and universities is that, even though they tend to draw their students from more advantaged socio-economic backgrounds, they promote diversity and provide useful competition for public institutions, especially at higher levels of education.

GOVERNMENT'S ROLE

There is a need to follow a mix of both public and private presence in the education sector. Public intervention in education has several advantages. It can reduce inequality, improve accessibility, compensate for market failures in lending for education and disseminate information about the benefits and availability of education.

Governments can help improve the quality of education by establishing standards, supporting inputs, adopting flexible strategies for the acquisition and use of inputs, and monitoring performance.

EQUITY

Achieving equity in education means that every citizen has the right to basic education that enables acquisition of basic knowledge and skills to function effectively in society. It also means that no qualified student is denied access to education because of an inability to pay. Ensuring equity in education requires both financial and administrative measures.

Financial measures, such as scholarships, are important at all levels to enable the poor to gain from education. Scholarships can cover fees and other direct costs, such as transport and uniforms and, when appropriate, can compensate families for the indirect costs of sending children to school - for example, loss of labour services for the household.

Administrative measures can increase enrolments of the poor, females and other deprived classes of society. Programs designed to demonstrate the importance of educating children can increase the demand for schooling among the poor.

COMPETITION

There is evidence that competition among schools improves their performance. For choice to be effective, the student must have more than one possible school. The institutions should have some distinguishing characteristics. For example, what aspects of the curriculum are emphasised, in teaching styles, and, at higher levels, in course offerings. Finally, institutions need to enjoy considerable autonomy in how they teach. The availability of a variety of institutions enables parents and students to exercise choice and thus gives institutions an incentive to adapt to demand.

AUTONOMY

Quality of education can benefit when schools have the autonomy to use instructional inputs according to local school and community conditions and are accountable to parents and communities. Fully autonomous institutions have authority to allocate their resources and they are able to create an educational environment adapted to local conditions inside and outside the school.

Accountable autonomous institutions can be encouraged by both administrative and financial means. Administrative measures include giving school management the authority to allocate resources - for example, the authority to deploy personnel and to alter such things as the timing of the school day and year and the language of instruction to fit local conditions. Most critically, teachers need to have the authority to determine classroom practices, within limits set by a broad national curriculum.

POLITICS

Education is intensely political: it affects the majority of citizens, involves all levels of government, and makes up a significant component of government spending. There are also public subsidies that are biased in favour of the elite. Prevailing systems of education spending and management often protect the interests of teachers and the government rather than those of parents, students, communities and the poor. Teachers, administrators, textbook publishers - all have reasons to prefer things to remain as they are, or to change only gradually.

DEMOCRACY

The concept of democracy has spread rapidly in the last decade. Local governments are becoming more important. Citizens are gaining an increasing voice through civil society organisations, community groups, religious organisations and chambers of commerce. If democracy is to survive, citizens must develop capabilities that require them to be well informed, understand the impact of issues, make wise choices and hold elected officials accountable for the responsibility thrust on them. Education is the process of enlarging people's choices. Choices that are created by expanding human capabilities- what people do and can do in their lives.

Globalisation and a shift to a market-led, knowledge-based economy demands that education must become the cornerstone of development if India has to find a place at the top of the league of nations.

Building knowledge for a competitive, information-based society must be the core theme of reforms in education.

Education, for girls as well as for boys, therefore deserves the highest priority on the government agenda - not just those of the Ministry of Human Resources Development.

Education must shape adaptable, competitive workers who can readily acquire new skills and innovate. Education must also support the continued expansion of knowledge.

It is important that skills, as a result of education, have economic value beyond their intrinsic merit. Equally, it is important that there is diversity in order to avoid an abundance in any one skill and consequent poor rewards. To illustrate, although computer skills are valuable, if too many computer specialists are produced, rewards for them will be weak.

An increase in aggregate spending on education is intuitively appealing, but should be treated cautiously as appreciable changes in education outcomes result only with relatively large shifts in spending. The accent must be on promoting efficient use of resources as much aş on expanding the overall resource envelope.

Efficiency is achieved by making public investments where they will yield the highest returns. This is in the area of primary education. Consequently, government investments to improve enrolments and retention in primary education must have the highest priority in intersectional allocation of educational resources.

Decisions about public education priorities beyond basic education must be taken within a broad sectoral approach. Once we have largely achieved universal primary and secondary education, then we can consider higher education as a priority.

There must be a concerted effort to free up resources for primary education through concomitant changes in other sectors and subsectors. This will mean reallocation of public spending to education from other sectors such as defence and inefficient public sector enterprises. It will also imply a gradual move to full cost recovery in higher education and encouraging the emergence of a largely self-financing private sector.

To achieve equity, the government must ensure that no qualified student is denied access to education because of an inability to pay.

Because the gap between private and social returns is larger for higher education than for basic education, students and parents must bear part of the costs of higher education.

Governments must encourage private financing by taking on some of the risks that makes financial institutions reluctant to lend for higher education.

A credit market for education, together with selective scholarships, especially in higher education, must be nurtured.

Concerted steps must be taken to harness new technology opportunities in content and delivery of education. Prudent steps must be taken to use already existing technology options, such as in communications, more effectively. Education systems must also gear for an era of cyber-age education without sacrificing the basic principles of elementary education and cognitive learning.

A climate of competition among educational institutions must be fostered.

Decentralising the management of public education and encouraging the expansion of private and community educational institutions must be given thrust.

SOCIO-ECONOMIC DEVELOPMENT OF WOMEN'S EDUCATION

In the Bahá'í teachings there are two extraordinary statements about the education of women. First, that women's education is of greater importance than men's education and, secondly, that not until the equality of opportunity in education for the two sexes is established will the foundations of war be removed. These challenging ideas deserve study in order for us to understand their meaning and ramifications.

The principle of sexual equality in education - one facet of the general principle of the equality of the sexes - was revolutionary when given by Bahá'u'lláh in the mid 1800s. It was set forth more than half a century before western thought added sexual equality to its list of rationally-based moral principles of relevance to political life, such as democracy, secularism, and the rights of the individual, and long before it became enshrined in numerous national and international documents as a politically correct, universal value.

The signs of the rapid convergence between the ideas of the secular world and the teachings of the Bahá'í Faith are abundant. In the political and economic spheres, for example, this is conspicuous presently in the enthusiasm for global governance among thinkers, academics, and international institutions. It can also be seen in the acceptance, among many influential opinion-makers, of the need for a world currency and for international economic policy coordination. Many other ideas and institutions prescribed by Bahá'u'lláh in the last century have been embraced by the world in the past few decades. The recognition of the wisdom of the Bahá'í emphasis on women's education is a recent addition to the list of areas of convergence.

Women's status

Women account for roughly half the world's population, perform two-thirds of the hours worked, receive one-tenth of the world's income, and have less than one hundredth of the world's property registered in their names. Female deprivation is particularly acute in the developing countries with high levels of poverty, though in affluent nations women also suffer low status due to conservative attitudes.

The most dramatic and telling statistic of women's status is the sex-ratio in the population, that is, the number of females per 100 males. It is a well-known fact that life-expectancy at birth favours females. This appears to be a biological constant. Yet, the proportion of females to males varies greatly across different regions of the world. For example, the proportion of females is 52.5% in the industrialised world but in sub-Saharan Africa women account for only 51% of the population. The figures are 48% of the population in East Asia and less than 47% in South Asia. From figures such as these, economist Amartya Sen has estimated that there are 100 million women "missing" in the world. Sen describes the fate of these women as "one of the more momentous problems facing the contemporary world." This is a moral as well as a development-related problem.

The overwhelming reason why 100 million women are missing in the world is excess female mortality. In the developed world, women outlive men by an average of six years; by contrast, in large parts of South Asia, men can expect to live longer than women. Differential mortality is only the most dramatic manifestation of systematic discrimination against females. Women and girls are more likely to be impoverished than men and boys. Also, studies have found that girls are fed less than their brothers and that their illnesses are less likely to be treated. It should come as no surprise then that, in most regions of the world, female literacy and education fall far short of male literacy and education, as shown in Table 1.

While poverty and cultural factors must surely influence the extent of female deprivation, they do not explain it entirely. For example, sub-Saharan Africa is one of the poorest regions of the world but the problem of excess mortality of females is much less severe there than in South Asia.

Table 1.
Male-Female Gaps in education, 1990 (Index: Males = 100)

Region	Adult Literacy	Primary enrolment	Secondary enrolment	Tertiary enrolment
Nordic countries	-	100	101	121
OECD	-	99	98	103
All Developing Countries	73	88	78	70
Least Developed Countries	57	84	67	44
Arab states	61	92	77	65
East Asia	80	96	79	73
Latin America and Caribbean	97	98	98	70
South Asia	55	75	60	48
SE Asia and the Pacific	90	97	95	73
Sub-Saharan Africa	66	85	72	46

Source: Human Development Report 1995

Equality of the sexes—in terms of men and women's command over resources, their access to education and health, and in terms of freedom to develop their potential—has an intrinsic value in its own right. The equal treatment of the sexes for intrinsic reasons is, in the parlance of welfare economics, the equity reason for reducing gender-imbalances. A second important reason in favour of reducing gender-imbalances is what might be termed the instrumental reason, that is, the gains to be had from granting equality.

For example, if with equal education, women's contribution to economic development (or to other desirable goals) is comparable to men's, then reducing gender-imbalances in education will enhance women's capacity to contribute to economic progress. This is the efficiency reason for reducing gender inequality in areas where women are currently deprived. Both the intrinsic (equity) and instrumental (efficiency) based reasons for gender equality are emphasised in the teachings of Bahá'u'lláh.

Economic efficiency

Human capital theory suggests that just as physical capital (machines) augments people's economic productivity, so human capital acquired through education improves the productivity of individuals. Studies of the sources of economic growth demonstrate persuasively that education plays a major role as a factor in the rise of output per worker. The new growth theories in economics place education and human resource development at the centre of their explanation for long-term economic growth.

Confidence has grown in the belief that education affects economic growth because many studies have shown the positive correlation between a country's educational effort and its economic status, and causality has been attributed to education. Prominent examples of this are the so-called "miracle" economies of East Asia. If female schooling raises human capital, productivity, and economic growth as much as male schooling does, then women's disadvantage in education is economically inefficient.

Research world-wide shows that, in general, the economic benefits from women's education - calculated as the economic rate of return to education - are comparable to those from men's education. Thus, from the point of view of economic efficiency, the gender gap in education is undesirable.

Social efficiency

While the economic benefits of educating girls are similar in size to the economic benefits of educating boys, recent findings suggest that the social benefits from investing in female education are far greater than those from investing in male education. Specifically, female education has powerful effects on the total fertility rate (and hence on population growth), the infant mortality rate, the female disadvantage in child survival, and on child health and nutrition. By contrast, statistical analyses show that male schooling has relatively much smaller effects on these important social outcomes.

For example, a recent study by Subbarao and Raney using national aggregate data from 72 countries regressed the total fertility rate of 1985 on the male and female secondary school enrolment rates lagged by 10 years, i.e. on the enrolment rates of 1975. The objective was to examine the effect of education on fertility, controlling for a number of other factors such as family planning service provision and per capita income. The results show that female secondary school enrolment is inversely correlated with the total fertility rate but that male secondary school enrolment shows no strong correlation. Similarly, a regression of the 1985 infant mortality rate on 10 year lagged male and female secondary school enrolment rates shows that while female education is associated with lower infant mortality, male education has no statistically significant effect.

Moreover, district per capita income, urbanisation, and the spread of medical facilities were not statistically significant determinants of total fertility rate. While these latter three variables do have positive effects on child survival levels, their effects were relatively small compared with the powerful effect of female literacy.

Numerous studies have been carried out using household-level data that confirm the findings from studies using aggregate data. To cite one example, an examination of the determinants of fertility in fourteen countries of sub-Saharan Africa by Ainsworth, Beegle, and Nyamete using household survey data shows an inverse correlation between female schooling and fertility in virtually all of the countries, though the relationship is non-linear: female primary schooling has an inverse relation with fertility in about half of the countries only but female secondary schooling is universally associated with lower fertility, and the strength of the correlation increases with increasing years of schooling.

Among ever-married women, husband's schooling has no significant relation with fertility in about one-third of the countries. Moreover, in cases where both women's and men's schooling matter, women's schooling exerts a much larger negative effect on fertility than men's schooling. Simulations show that the benefits from expanding female education are far greater than the benefits from other public interventions such as improving family planning service provision or increasing the number of physicians in the population.

For example, Subbarao and Raney found that a doubling of the 1975 average secondary school enrolment ratio in the 72 sample countries from 19% to 38% would have reduced the average number of births in 1985 by 29% compared to the actual number in 1985, whereas a doubling of the family planning provision would have reduced the number of births by only 3.5%.

The gains in terms of deaths averted are also striking. Simulations predict that doubling the female secondary school enrolment ratio from 19% to 38% in 1975 reduces infant deaths in 1985 by 64% while doubling the number of physicians reduces the number of infant deaths by a mere 2.5%. Doubling per capita income (or GDP) from the average of $650 in the 72 sample countries to $1300 would have no effect on the number of infant deaths! Subbarao and Raney also reported data on desired family size from the World Fertility Survey for 37 countries. Econometric analysis of this data suggested that after controlling for per capita income, female secondary school enrolment was a highly significant determinant of desired family size (and therefore of the total fertility rate and population growth rate). Male school enrolment ratio, however, had no impact on desired family size.

Finally, a large body of microeconomic evidence shows that increases in women's education generally lead to increases in their labour force participation as well as in their earnings. Educated women's greater participation in labour market work and their higher earnings are thought to be good for their own status (economic models say "bargaining power") within the household, and are good for their children because it appears that a greater proportion of women's income than men's is spent on child goods.

On the down side, it may be thought that educated women's greater labour force participation takes them away from their children for longer periods of time (than is the case for uneducated or less educated women) and this may disadvantage educated women's children through neglect. At present this is a relatively unresearched issue. However, limited evidence suggests that children whose mothers work have just as good or better educational outcomes than children whose mothers do not work.

PATHWAYS TO FEMALE EDUCATION

Economists tend to focus on the role of incentives as a way of understanding phenomena. They reason that female education lowers the fertility rate by reducing desired family size and that this, in turn, is because education raises the value of women's economic activities by raising the labour market rewards from going out of the home for work. In other words, the opportunity-cost of staying at home for child bearing and rearing increases as women become more educated and, so, educated women desire smaller families.

Education may also change women's preferences about the quantity versus the quality of children, with educated women choosing fewer children but of better "quality". Moreover, as mentioned earlier, recent research suggests that a greater proportion of women's cash income than men's is spent on child goods, so that women's education and the consequent increase in women's income would appear to have particular benefits for child quality.

Education of women improves child health because of educated mothers' greater knowledge of the importance of hygiene and of simple remedies. All this lowers infant mortality, which in turn means that a family does not need to have a large number of children in order to hedge against the possibility of premature death of some children. Further, it appears that education of females increases the age at marriage (or at cohabitation) and through this delay, lowers the total fertility rate, i.e. number of children ever born to a woman.

Finally, some studies find that mother's education has a greater impact on the educational attainment and school achievement of children than father's education. This is plausible given the greater interaction between mother and children in most families since, in most countries, fathers are usually the main earners in the household. In this way, education of females contributes more significantly (than the education of males) to increases in human capital, productivity, and economic growth not only in their own generation but also in the next generation.

Gender equality in education

It appears that there is an increasing challenge to the principle of gender equality not only from religious fundamentalists but also from a broader current, particularly in Asia, that questions the universality of the principle, contesting it as a "western value". For example, when a recent study found that Pakistan had forgone much economic growth between 1970 and 1985 because of its large scale failure to invest in the education of its females, a large group of angry Pakistani economics academics called education of females a "western value" and argued that education of females had led to increased incidence of divorce, family breakdown and social problems in western countries.

4

SCHOOL COMMUNITY

In ancient times, India was a great centre for learning. The 500 years from the 4th century AD to the close of the 8th century under the Guptas and Vardhanas was a glorious period in the history of Indian education. It was an age of the Nalanda and Valabhi Universities and the rise of Indian sciences, mathematics and astronomy. The Nalanda University had 1,500 teachers and thousands of students, maintained by revenues from more than 100 villages. Its fame attracted scholars from all over the world. Its open system covered vedas, logic, grammar, Buddhist and Hindu philosophy, astronomy and medicine. Sadly, today India does not enjoy that glory in the field of education.

CURRENT STATE OF EDUCATION

In 1997, India had an education index of 0.54 (maximum=1) against an average 0.95 enjoyed by countries with high human development. The education index is a construct that is a function of gross enrolment in education and adult literacy, and has been brought out by United Nations Development Programme. China is far ahead with an index of 0.78; Sri Lanka has an index of 0.82. Even Swaziland, Botswana and Namibia have much higher indices of 0.76, 0.73 and 0.81. The primary net enrolment ratio as percent of relevant age group was 77.2 percent. The secondary net enrolment ratio as percent of relevant age group drops alarmingly to 59.7 percent. The adult literacy rate is 54%.

Between 1993 and 1996, India spent 3.4 percent of its GNP on public education, constituting 11.6 percent of total government expenditure. Countries like Canada and Sweden spent 7 percent and 8.3 percent of their GNP on education. Among the relatively less developed countries, Swaziland, Namibia and Botswana spent 7.3 percent, 9.1 percent and 10.4 percent of their GNP on education. India shows a high gender gap in education. Female adult literacy stands at just 39.4 percent, just 59 percent of the male rate. Female primary net enrolment ratio stands at 71, while female secondary net enrolment ratio drops to 48. Female adult literacy is far higher in countries like Indonesia (79.5 percent), Swaziland (76.3 percent), Namibia (78.5 percent), Gabon (56.8 percent), Zambia (67.5 percent), Malawi (43.4 percent), Rwanda (55.6 percent) and Lesotho (92.5 percent).

Even after 53 years of independence, we have not been able to achieve the dream of eradicating illiteracy. In 1942, the British Government instituted the Sargent Committee to propose a plan for eradicating illiteracy in India. The committee proposed a plan that would make India 100 % literate in 40 years. Indian nationalists scoffed at the plan stating that India does not have that kind of patience, and wanted quicker results. However, 58 years after that and 53 years after independence, our literacy rate is only 62 %. It must be noted that there has been considerable progress in the field of education in India.

The literacy rate has increased from 18.3% in 1951 to 62% in 1997. The number of primary schools increased from 2.09 lakhs in 1950-51 to 6.1 lakhs in 1998. The enrolment in schools increased from about 240 lakhs in 1950-51 to about 1090 lakhs in 1998. The student enrolment in universities and colleges increased from about 2 lakhs at the time of independence to 56 lakhs in 1998. India has 46% of its population aged 15 years and above as illiterates. In contrast,

China spends only 2.6% of its GNP on education but has only 22% of its population aged 15 years and above as illiterates. About one third of the world's illiterates are in India.

NATIONAL POLICY ON EDUCATION

The National Policy on Education (NPE), framed in 1986 and amended in 1992, accords priority to universalisation of elementary education, universal retention of children up to 14 years of age, non-formal education in the educationally backward states and thrust to the National Literacy Mission. It states that " the investment on education be gradually increased to reach a level of 6% of the National Income as early as possible". In fact, several Government documents dating back to 1969 state this goal. The actual level of investment has remained far short of this target.

The Programme of Action of the NPE 1986 and as revised in 1992 states "Time is of essence, and unless we act now, we stand in the danger of once again missing the opportunity of education reform, so critical not only for the development of our nation, but for our very survival". It also mentions that "it is people's achievement in the education reconstruction which will make the real difference" We have not yet succeeded in any meaningful reform and also having society's involvement in the process.

Pre-primary Education

Primary education is the building block for developing literacy. However, the transition from home to the school environment poses a significant challenge to children. Moreover, scientific research has found that language skills, intelligence, personality and social behaviour are largely determined by age four or five. The need for a pre primary school was therefore felt to prepare the child mentally, physically and socially for the many years of education to be pursued ahead. Primary education in

India is characterised by two extremes. In rural areas, it is common that children who have studied for as long as six years lack the basic reading and writing skills, while children in urban areas are subjected to extreme pressures to excel in academic skills.

The root of this dichotomy lies in pre-primary education system in India. While the pre-primary school in the rural schools rarely stresses on education, children in urban areas attend as much as two to three years of pre-school. In rural India in 1984, 124 of every thousand children born to illiterate mothers died before age one. In the same rural areas in 1991, about 64 percent of children under three exhibited some level of malnutrition. And of the 101 million Indian children enrolled in primary school in 1991-92, the dropout rate was 47%. To improve the situation, the Indian government initiated Integrated Child Development Services (ICDS) in 1975. ICDS is supported by the World Food Programme, Centre for American Relief Everywhere, UNICEF, the European Union, USAID and the World Bank.

The first and second ICDS projects attempt to combine education with basic services to children, pregnant women and nursing mothers. It is the largest such programme in the world, aimed at seventeen million pre-school children and seven million pregnant and nursing women. The programme is delivered at the village level in four States: Andhra Pradesh, Orissa, Madhya Pradesh and Bihar and gives priority to the low-income groups. The two projects work through a network of Anganwadi ("courtyard") centres, each run by an Anganwadi worker, usually selected from the local village. The Anganwadi workers gather between 20 and 40 children in a courtyard for several hours each weekday and provide non-formal pre-school education, supplementary feeding, immunisations, health check ups and medical referral services. They also provide health and nutrition education, parenting education through home visits and maternal and child health referrals.

The projects use existing services of diverse governmental departments and of voluntary agencies, but overall administration responsibilities lie with the Department of Women and Child Development within the Ministry of Human Resources Development. Though the ICDS has now spread to almost all states, most of the Anganwadi centres operate at a minimum level of quality and estimates are that only 12% of India's children are reached by any early childhood assistance.

Primary Education

Provision of free and compulsory education to all the children until they complete the age of 14 years is a Directive Principle of the Constitution. The stated national goal of education for all has still not been met. India has steadily raised primary enrolment rates since Independence and today has the world's second largest education system after China, with 1080 lakhs children aged 6-10 attending primary school. Yet, one of its most stubborn development challenges is the fact that about 330 lakhs children of primary school age are still not enrolled in school. In addition, the qualities of teaching and retention power of primary schools are weak, and there are large gaps in access to education, quality of education and learning according to gender, ethnicity and location.

Though the gross enrolment rate in primary schools is about 90%, there are still about 33 lakhs children who are not enrolled in any school and the total number of illiterates in 1997 was about 3000 lakhs. The attendance ratio and survival rate makes the picture even more dismal. India's primary school survival rate of 62% is also lower than other developing countries such as Brazil (71%), Mexico (84%) and Egypt (98%). This indicates that very few students are reaching the fifth or sixth grade. Dropout rates measured by the Department of Education show that 35% of males and 39% of females dropout before completing primary education. Only 84% of rural habitations have access to a school within a distance of 1 km and only 76% have access to a school within a distance of 3km, though in terms of population, the figures are higher at 95% and 85% respectively. 21000 schools are still single teacher schools.

The quality of education imparted leaves much to be desired, with students not being able to read and write even in the fifth grade. This is due to the fact that availability of a school does not mean it has all the required facilities. The spending on primary education as a percentage of total public expenditure in the same period in India was 40 %. Fifteen other emerging nations were compared with India, and India's percentage spend is the second lowest ahead of Peru.

A study of China shows that due to a compulsory 6 year and 9 year education system, the enrolment percentage is in the high 90s for the age group 6-11. China, whose literacy rate was less than 20 % in the late 40s has gone up substantially to over 80 % today. China has achieved all this in a matter of 40 to 50 years. It is not difficult for India to outdo China in a shorter time span. A phased drive called Operation Blackboard has been launched to improve the basic infrastructure of primary education. Till 1989-90 a total of Rs 383 crores had been spent under the scheme. The education policy provides for opening of residential schools for talented children. These schools are named Navodaya Vidyalayas. These schools are residential, co-educational and primarily for children from rural areas. At least one third seats are reserved for girls. Presently, the overall percentages of SC/ST students admitted so far are 21% and 12% respectively. The Navodaya Vidyalayas aim to provide opportunities to the talented children to develop their full potential and to promote national integration. Education in these schools is free for all students. It is proposed to open such schools in each district in the country. 342 Navodaya Vidyalayas covering 24 States and 6 Union Territories have been set up till 31st January 1994.

Secondary Education

The Secondary Education which serves as a bridge between primary and higher education is expected to prepare young persons between the age group 14-18 in the world of work and entry into higher education. The children population at the secondary and senior secondary level, as projected in 1996-97 by NSSO has been estimated at 966 lakhs. There are over one lakh secondary/higher schools and two lakhs upper primary schools in the country. In spite of the rapid increase in the number of schools, there are still unserved areas in the country where there is no secondary/higher school for 10 to 20 kms.

Against this population, the enrolment figures of the 1997-98 shows that only 270 lakhs are attending schools. Thus, two-third of the eligible population remains out of the school system. To accommodate the children in schools at the secondary level, we have at present 1.10 lakh institutions (1998-99). With the emphasis on universalisation of elementary education, the enrolment is bound to increase and once this universalisation takes place, we may require more than two lakhs institutions at the secondary level to accommodate them. There are several systems of education at the secondary level. Each state has its own board of secondary education.

In addition, there are the Central Board of Secondary Education (CBSE) and Indian Council for Secondary Education (ICSE). The Central Board of Secondary Education (CBSE) was set up in its present form in 1952 with an objective to promote national integration to provide uniform school education in the country, cutting across state borders and linguistic barriers. CBSE has affiliated schools all over the country and even abroad. CBSE has also set up an Open School in 1979 for propagation of distance education in the country. The National Council of Educational Research & Training (NCERT) was established in 1961 to assist and advise the Ministry of Education and Culture in implementing policies and programmes in the field of education. The Council, with the objective of bringing about national integration in education, has over the years revised secondary level syllabi and textbooks in collaboration with the CBSE. It also conducts national surveys of teacher education every five years and organises training for school teachers.

Higher Education

India has one of the largest 'Higher Education Systems' in the world. It has 237 Universities, 10600 Colleges, 41 Deemed universities, 70.78 lakh students 3.31 lakh teachers. There are several organisations involved in the field of higher education system in the country. They include:

University Grants Commission (UGC) is responsible for co-ordination, determination and maintenance of standards and release of grants. Professional Councils are responsible for recognition of courses, promotion of professional institutions and providing grants to undergraduate programmes and various awards. The statutory professional councils are:

— All India Council for Technical Education (AICTE)

— Distance Education Council (DEC)

— Indian Council for Agriculture Research (ICAR)

— Bar Council of India (BCI),

— National Council for Teacher Education (NCTE)

— Rehabilitation Council of India (RCI)

— Medical Council of India (MCI),

— Pharmacy Council of India (PCI)

— Indian Nursing Council (INC)

— Dentist Council of India (DCI)

— Central Council of Homeopathy (CCH)

— Central Council of Indian Medicine (CCIM)

The central government is responsible for major policy relating to higher education in the country. It provides grants to the UGC and establishes central universities in the country. The Central Government is also responsible for declaration of Educational Institutions as 'Deemed to be University' on the recommendation of the UGC. Presently there are sixteen central universities in the country. In pursuance of the Mizoram Accord, another Central University in the State of Mizoram is planned. There are 37 Institutions which have been declared as Deemed to be Universities by the Govt. of India as per Section 3 of the UGC Act, 1956.

State governments are responsible for establishment of State Universities and colleges, and provide plan grants for their development and non-plan grants for their maintenance. The co-ordination and co-operation between the Union and the States is brought about in the field of education through the Central Advisory Board of Education (CABE). Education is on the 'Concurrent list' subject to Entry 66 in the Union List of the Constitution. This gives exclusive Legislative Power to the Central Govt. for co-ordination and determination of standards in Institutions of higher education or research and scientific and technical institutions.

Professional Education

Professional education would cover engineering and technical education, medical education, management, financial and law courses. Professional education has great potential for adding value to products and service for contributing to the national economy and improving the quality of life of the people. The Indian technical education system is accorded a great deal of respect based on the alumni who have been setting trail-blazing paths in the developing countries. The large number of Indians who are being sought after by developed countries and large multinationals in various spheres such as information technology, financial services, marketing, medicine etc. is testimony of the innate strength of our technical education system.

There is however a view that this is a reflection of the innate ability of Indian brainpower and has little to do with the education system. We need to rejuvenate the system by modernisation and removal of obsolescence of the curriculum. A large number of inventions and discoveries all over the world have been the result of research initiatives in educational institutions. However, India is an exception to this. There is a felt need to foster a strong culture of research with much stronger linkages with the industry and societal needs.

The colleges and universities have largely bypassed the rural sector, except a few universities designated as rural universities. India is still a largely rural nation. It is the duty of the education system to disseminate knowledge to the entire nation. The urban-centric approach has left a large population of the country untouched. These institutions should utilise the reach of the latest medium and also spearhead the transfer of technology to the rural sector.

Adult Education

The relationship between adult education and the basic education process is one of interdependence. Recognising the vital role of adult education in the social development of the country, many policies and policy provisions have reflected the Government's concern and commitment for promotion of adult education. Since independence, the Government has been making serious efforts to achieve 100% literacy but it has remained an elusive goal, due to several factors, such as economic constraints, unchecked growth population, lack of community participation, lack of awareness etc.

The literacy rate at present is 62% against the population growth rate of 2 %. Various programs have been launched in the country to enhance literacy rate through six months programme and basic education. Simultaneously efforts are being made to support adult illiterates with daily life skills and knowledge. The horizon of adult education has widely expanded in the national scenario during the last two decades. Of the various factors which have influenced its development, the launching of the National Adult Education Programme (NAEP) in 1978 and the National Literacy Mission (NLM) in 1988 have been greatly responsible for catapulting adult education into a national programme of high priority and prominence besides ensuring it committed policy support and liberal grants from the Government of India.

Today, several types of adult education activities viz.; Total Literacy Campaigns (TLC), post literacy and continuing education programs and experimental projects like Mahila Samakhya are being implemented in different parts of India by official agencies, Non-Governmental Organisations (NGO) and educational institutions. The operationalisation of these diverse programs have not only generated a variety of professional literature ranging from literacy primers, post literacy materials, training manuals, evaluation reports, research studies and innumerable articles but also led to the expansion of training programs. The systematic strategies evolved by the NLM towards developing the administrative and academic infrastructure at national, state and district levels has been duly supported by the University Grants Commission's (UGC).

UGC has established 92 University Departments of Adult Continuing Education, which has also played an important role in strengthening the professional base of adult education in the country. Although literacy levels are low, there has been progress in improving attainment for both sexes in India over the last several decades. In 1981, 70% of women and 43% of men were illiterate. By 1997 this figure had come down to 50% for women and 27% for men. Thus there has been an increase in the proportion of women who are literate in just about 15 years. Despite the improvements in literacy, there continues to be a large gap between the literacy levels of men and of women.

Additionally, there are differences in literacy rate by place of residence, with rates in rural areas lagging behind rates in urban areas. In 1991, the urban female literacy rate was more than twice that of rural rate, 64 and 31 percent respectively. While there have, however, been substantial increase in literacy rates in both urban and rural areas, the gap between the two sectors has not narrowed appreciably. The difference in literacy rates among the states is also extreme. Mizoram has the highest female literacy rate, with 95% of women literate in 1997. The state with the second highest female literacy is Kerala, where nearly 90% of women are literate.

On the other hand, there are several states that have literacy rates of less than 40%, including Bihar and Uttar Pradesh, the two most populous states. As with India as a whole, many states have large rural-urban differences in female literacy. In 6 of the 24 states, 25% or less of the women in rural areas are literate. In Rajasthan, less than 12% of rural women are literate. The Total Literacy Campaigns, constituting the principal strategy for eradication of illiteracy, have been extended to cover 282 districts and the Post Literacy Campaigns to 105 districts. The focus of the campaigns has now shifted to Hindi speaking States having bulk of the illiterate population. A significant event in 1988 was the setting up of a National Literacy Authority to manage the national literacy missions aimed at achieving 80% literacy in the 15-35 age group in the country by 1995. A total of 58.07 million people have been enrolled under various National Literacy Missions as in August,1994.

Women's Literacy

It is believed that when you educate a man you educate an individual but when you educate a woman you educate the family. The development of a nation cannot only be assured through the technological and materialistic advances, but also through the quality of life. The current framework of National

Development recognises women as one who can and has played a crucial role in social reforms economic development and also in the political process. Women make the most effective providers of healthcare, non-formal teacher and managers of the local environments. As a wife and mother, she is the most influential member in determining the stability of her family and the development of her children's personality. Hence, the women's development is a pre requisite for the all round development of the society.

Many studies have shown that there is a strong correlation between several developmental indicators and level of literacy of the population. Such correlation is particularly strong with the level of female education. It is found that the relation between the age of marriage of a girl and her achievement in education is positive. On the other hand infant mortality rate, birth rate and total fertility rate are negatively correlated. The lower the educational level of the mother, the more number of children born to her and greater is the risk of reproductive mortality/ morbidity. In today's technological worlds education, especially for women is much more important for reduced population growth. Literacy levels are highly correlated with the health status of the population.

Kerala has the lowest infant mortality rates and the highest life expectancies of all the states. Conversely, Uttar Pradesh and Bihar have some of the lowest life expectancies found in India. A woman's lack of education also has a negative impact on the health and well-being of her children. Recent surveys have found that infant mortality was inversely related to a mother's educational level. Also, children of illiterate mothers are twice as likely to be undernourished or stunted as compared to children whose mothers have completed at least high school. Of the literate women in India, 59% have only a primary education or less. This level of education may not be sufficient to meaningfully improve the status of these women. Only 41% of the literate population, or 13% of all Indian women, have more than a primary education.

Pre-primary Education

Issues

1. *Social equity*: Poor children face many problems in their childhood years, such as lack of nutrition, stunted mental development and reluctance to study. These attributes later lead to low achievement, high dropout rates and functional illiteracy. Pre-primary school can tackle these critical deficiencies early and build a strong base for the child's successful learning.
2. *Socio-economic*: Early childhood education increases the productivity of a child and in turn increases the probability of the child's success at school. In the later years, this may reduce social costs in areas such as school repetition and health education.
3. *Increasing literacy*: Early child development programmes combine the objectives of education with health and nutrition. Pre-primary schools are mostly in the form of 'day care centres' where children are taken care of and provided with the necessary minimum nutrition. Many children and women don't attend school because they have to take care of their siblings or children. The pre-primary school thus gives them some free time, which they can use to attend school themselves and improve literacy.
4. Increasing productivity: Female participation in the labour force throughout the developing world is substantial and increasing. Availability of childcare centres, which provides education and health, can increase the productivity and income of self- employed women and creates opportunities for additional learning and education.

Imperatives for Sectoral Planning

While the dichotomy between urban and rural pre-primary education has to be eliminated, the pre-primary education system needs to change focus from academics to all round development of children. This calls for a radical change in teaching methodology based on scientific principles. Research has shown that exposing young children to interesting sources of information for very brief periods each day stimulates the development of the brain cells during early years and fosters a spontaneous curiosity and natural love of learning in children. The pre-primary education system should be based on these scientific principles and has to focus on developing a conducive atmosphere for learning and stimulating the innate curiosity of children.

Learning should be in the form of presenting information to the child in an interesting manner and inducing the child to inquire about the subject. There should not be undue emphasis on memorising. Active teaching should be confined to brief periods and not extend beyond the child's span of interest. The teacher should engage in active teaching to a group of around five children while other children are engaged in play and other activities. Since the child has a natural tendency to learn languages, very high importance should be given to development of basic reading and writing skills in different languages.

Primary Education

Issues

a. *Urban-rural divide*: Education is largely perceived as urban-centric. The stark difference in the literacy rates between rural and urban areas underline this point. In 1997, the urban literacy percentage was 80 % whereas the rural literacy percentage was only 56 %. Apart from the large difference in the literacy percentages, there is a vast quality difference in primary education between the rural and urban areas. This glaring disparity results in fewer opportunities for rural students in the higher education streams. Distance between schools and the students is high in certain states especially in the rural areas, which reflects in the educational backwardness of the states. Compared to the urban areas, the availability of trained teachers in the rural areas is limited.

b. *Teaching methodology*: The current system emphasises teaching by rote. The students are not exposed to experiential learning. This curtails the innate spirit of the children to learn through experiments and practical situations.

c. *Low enrolment and high dropout rates*: Primary school enrolment and attendance ratios are the most common indicators to measure the success of a primary education system. Net primary school enrolment ratios describe the percentage of primary school-age children who are registered in school. Primary school attendance ratios estimate the percentage of primary school-age children that are actually attending school. Another important indication of success of a school system is the student retention rate, which gives the percentage of enrolled children who reach a certain grade level. A comparison of these indicators with other developing countries shows that India fairs poorly on all the counts and the goal of universal primary education is still far beyond reach. Countries such as Bangladesh, Brazil, Egypt, Kenya, Nepal, Peru, Philippines, South Africa and Tanzania score over India in at least one of the two factors.

d. *Gender*: A major concern is the gender and caste wise disparity in literacy. Girls face many obstacles in pursuing education, including the traditional attitudes about female roles and a lack of female teachers. They are often expected to make a critical contribution to household work and childcare. With the result, girls constitute two-thirds of all children not attending school. The female literacy rate was 50% as compared to 73% for male in 1997. There are also wide variations among the various states, ranging from 90% female literacy in Kerala to 34% female literacy in Bihar. A similar situation prevails in the case of male literacy, which ranges from 96% in Kerala to 62% in Bihar.

e. *Myths about education*: The most common reasons given for inadequate spread of education are:

— Illiterate parents don't value education

— Children cannot attend school due to work

However, a recent survey carried out by a group of researchers based at the Delhi School of Economics and the Indian Social Institute finds otherwise. The survey covered all the schooling facilities in a randomly selected sample of 188 villages in Bihar, Madhya Pradesh, Uttar Pradesh and Rajasthan. The survey's findings have been released as part of the Public Report on Basic Education for India (PROBE), which is supported by the Centre for Development Economics (India).

Most respondents were very keen to enable their children to acquire education. 80.2 per cent of parents felt primary education should be made compulsory for all children. While 98 per cent stressed it was important for sons to go to school, as many as 89 per cent felt similarly in case of daughters. A small minority did not consider it important for a girl to be educated. While many children have to work long hours, the survey found that among children who don't attend school, about half worked less than three hours on the preceding day, and 33% had not worked at all during school hours on that day. Only 18% worked for more than eight hours. Also, girls worked more than boys did, but mainly at home. It is thus clear that the real causes go deeper than the apparent.

f. *Lack of Educational Infrastructure and Services*: One of the main reasons for India's poor progress in primary education is the lack of educational infrastructure and facilities. Overcrowded classrooms, long distances to schools, high student-to-teacher ratios, lack of school supplies such as desks, chairs, chalk, and blackboards etc. limit access to primary education.

g. *Cost of education*: Despite attempts to make primary education free for all, schooling is still a costly proposition for the average agricultural labourer. The PROBE survey estimates the cost incurred to send a child to a government primary school at Rs.366 per student per year. Sending two children to school amounts to about 30 to 40 days wages for an agricultural labourer. Further, the loss of the child's earnings and his job experience adds to the family's decision not to send children to school.

h. *Low teacher to student ratio*: During the period 1951 to 1997, the number of primary teachers increased by three times and the percentage of trained teachers has increased from 61% to 87%. However, the student teacher ratio has remained stable at around 45 students to a teacher. The actual number in states varies from 17 in Sikkim to 78 in Bihar. The PROBE survey found that there were about 50 children enrolled for each teacher. Teachers are often absent and spend little time in active teaching even when they are present. Further, the distribution of teachers among schools is highly uneven. This often leads to the actual pupil-teacher ratio being much higher than 50 in many schools, even shooting up to three-digit figures in some cases.

Another manifestation of this problem is that of the single-teacher school. Officially, single-teacher schools have been abolished in the country since introduction of Operation Blackboard in 1986. However, in the PROBE survey sample villages, 12 per cent of all primary schools had a single teacher appointed. Another 21 per cent had a single teacher present, because the other teachers were absent. Thus, one-third of all schools effectively had a single teacher.

i. *Inefficient teaching methods*: It is found that many children are unable to read and write even after many years of schooling. This is due to the inefficient teaching methods employed in schools. Teaching aids are rarely used either because they are not available or are kept locked up and away from the children. The favoured teaching method is copying from the board or from textbooks and emphasis is on controlling the children rather than teaching. Teachers are compelled to teach more than one grade at a time. Some teachers deal with this by concentrating their efforts on the higher grades, leaving the younger children to their own devices.

j. *Child labour*: The 1991 census of India lists 112.8 lakhs child workers in the age group of 5-14, 90% of which are in rural areas. Besides, 62 lakhs children are involved in housework, majority (88%) of which are girls. There is a strong relationship between child labour and lack of primary education. Working children have low enrolment, high absenteeism and dropout rates. This may be attributable to fatigue from long hours of labour, injuries and illnesses, and work schedules that conflict with school hours. Recognising this, the International Labour Organisation (ILO) has stipulated that the minimum working age should be more than the age required to complete compulsory education and in any event, not less than 15 years. However, India does not have any compulsory education laws.

The U.S. Department of Labour through its International Child Labour Programme has studied 16 developing countries to find the link between primary education and child labour. The fifth report in this series states that high absenteeism and drop out rates are particularly chronic among working children in rural areas. Though many countries have complementary child labour and compulsory education laws, India has no national laws in this regard. Only 14 states in India have legislation regarding compulsory education.

Imperatives for Sectoral Planning

There should be a compulsory enrolment of children at the age of 5 in primary schools. This should be enshrined in the constitution. A system of reward and penalty needs to be followed. The students should be offered incentives such as mid-day meals, free textbooks and teaching aids. There should be stiff penalties for parents in case the children are not admitted to schools. To ensure retention, the mid-day meal scheme and other incentives should continue. There are a large number of NGOs working in the field of primary education. The synergy between the Government and the NGOs should be utilised.

The curriculum should be overhauled to encourage learning through experience and not by rote. The teacher's role should shift to that of a facilitator. The trained teachers should serve a specified period in the rural areas, as in the banking system and the medical profession. A national education fund needs to be created. The donations to this fund should be offered attractive tax breaks. This fund to be utilised for primary education and adult literacy. There should be at least one primary school within 2 kms. of each prospect student.

The reach of new technology tools such as television, cable television and Internet should be utilised for enhancing the reach and quality of primary education. Economic incentives alone are not very effective in increasing school attendance. However, a recent survey carried out by ILO has found it to be very effective when combined with other social measures such as raising community awareness about education and improving educational quality and infrastructure. Economic incentives are thus very important in raising education levels and should be employed in India more as a means to offset the income loss incurred by sending a child to school. Incentives can be in the form of free meals to students, food to the student's family and free uniforms and books.

A variety of programs to provide alternative education opportunities for working and underprivileged children should be introduced. These may include the following programmes:

Orientation Schools: Temporary schools, which would operate in the lean months of employment, should be introduced. These schools should target working children who are early drop outs or have never attended school and should impart basic reading and writing skills, vocational skills and other skills relevant to their work environment. Focus should be on generating interest in the formal education system. Andhra Pradesh, with the highest number of working children in India, is implementing such a program successfully with about 74% of the students subsequently enrolling to formal schools.

Flexible Schedules: Another strategy for increasing school enrolment and attendance is to make school schedules more flexible, allowing working children the opportunity to both work and study. Schools should operate on a two-shift basis, one starting in the morning and other later in the day. Working children should be allowed the flexibility to attend school in either shift. Agricultural and rural labour requirements are highly seasonal. The school calendar should be adapted so that majority of the curriculum is covered in the lean months. Moreover, many labourers migrate to other places for some time in a year. Appropriate arrangements should be made to allow children of such labourers to attend school at different locations in the same grade. Such programmes have been successfully implemented in countries like Guatemala, Peru, Brazil and Mexico.

There should be national legislation requiring compulsory education for children during the ages of 6-14. Effective child labour laws fixing the minimum working age at 15 should complement this. An example of a country where compulsory education has worked to reduce child labour and increase literacy is Sri Lanka. The Sri Lankan government decided to enforce compulsory education in the 1920's and 1930's. With this compulsory education policy, school participation rates rose from 58 percent in 1946 to 74 percent in 1963. The literacy rate also increased from 58 percent in 1946 to 86 percent in 1984 and to 90% in 1997. Correspondingly, the employment rate of children in the ten to fourteen age group has shown a substantial decline from 13% in 1946 to 6.2% in 1963 and currently stands at 5.3% for males and 4.6% for females

Secondary Education

Issues

a. *Urban-rural divide*: The enrolment figures though improving with time, is still lopsided in favour of the urban areas. The distance to the nearest school is quite high especially in rural areas.

b. *Lack of facilities*: Most of the existing schools have poor facilities for laboratories, learning resources, computers and sports. The variance in the quality of teaching is stark between different schools. Apart from the lack of facilities, the other major reason for this is the lack of adequate teaching professionals in remote areas.

c. *Different systems*: There are several organisations administering to this education system both at the Centre and the states.

Imperatives for Sectoral Planning

A common system of education across the nation is absolutely necessary. This could contain common syllabi across the nation allowing for regional variations. The states would be responsible for implementing the syllabi. The curriculum should provide vocational education at the 10 + 2 levels. The curriculum to be reviewed periodically. All higher secondary and high schools to be provided computers at a ratio of at least 1 computer for every 50 students. Stress should be on practical learning rather than on theoretical learning.

Higher Education

Issues

As with the other sectors, there is a tremendous variance in the quality of education being imparted by various institutions. The reasons for these include the variation in infrastructure facilities in different institutions and variable quality of the teaching professionals. There are no innovations in teaching and research. The existing scheme for continuous learning of faculty is inadequate. The outcome is ill-equipped faculty members. The higher education is an urban phenomenon with most of the Universities located in the urban areas. Also the decision making process of the Universities is extremely slow. This is one of the reasons for the perception amongst the rural population that they do not need higher education.

The content and curriculum is not in tune with the needs of the society and does not reflect the changing trends. The result is an increasing level of educated unemployed. The objective of higher education at the most basic level is to prepare its students for employment. This would mean value addition of a fairly high level. However, as mentioned earlier this is merely a dream. The value addition for the cost of collegiate education is disproportionate. At the higher education level, the financing options for the students is almost non-existent. This and the other issues discussed above preclude a large segment of the Indian population from being a part of the higher education system.

Imperatives for Sectoral Planning

The system should provide affordable and quality higher education on par with the best in the world to all. This would mean tremendous value addition for the students and they would be better prepared for employment. There is a need to evaluate the utility of current Arts and Science courses in the prevailing scenario. This evaluation should not restrict to the curriculum alone but also to the linkage to employment opportunities.

There should be in-built mechanisms to constantly upgrade and evaluate curriculum. These evaluations should be undertaken at a maximum interval of one year. The private institutions should be encouraged to establish science and technology institutions. There should be no funding from Government to these institutions. The linkages between industry and academic institutions, especially in research and development, should be institutionalised.

All courses from the UG level should have a module on entrepreneurship. Continuous learning should be made mandatory for all teachers in higher education on a period basis. This should be at least 6 weeks of training for every two years of teaching. The institutions should be rated by independent agencies, as is done in the financial markets. The process should be analogous to the credit rating for financial instruments. All institutions failing the minimal quality tests to be given a pre-specified time to improve, failing which these are de-recognised. All institutions should obtain this rating each year. This should be prominently displayed in all communication and application forms. This would strengthen the accreditation process.

The University governance structure should be compact and effective. In view of global participation of the Universities, the issue concerning their jurisdiction of geographical territory needs a review. Also the University should be allowed to establish their centres of studies at various locations in India and abroad. The University administration should be effectively decentralised and based on the latest information technology techniques. The courses of studies should be flexible to encourage the students to choose the variety of subjects in tune with their strengths and the market demands. The University system should establish transfer of credits to enable students to move from one institution to the other.

Professional Education

Issues

The colleges and universities have largely bypassed the rural sector, except a few universities designated as rural universities. India is still a largely rural nation. It is the duty of the education system to disseminate knowledge to the entire nation. The urban-centric approach has left a large population of the country untouched. These institutions should utilise the reach of the latest medium and also spearhead the transfer of technology to the rural sector.

The faculty, once they are part of the academic system do not keep themselves abreast of the latest happenings in their field. There should be methods to compulsorily train teachers at specified periodicity. This would enable them to update themselves on the latest tools and techniques especially in the emerging areas. There is a variance of quality of education amongst institutions, with the result that for a few colleges and institutions, there is a greater demand for admissions, and for some others there are not enough requests for admissions. The cost of professional education is quite high. The lack of financing options attenuates this.

Imperatives for Sectoral Planning

An all-India examination for professional courses on the lines of SAT, GMAT or GRE should be organised. This will be the evaluation criterion for entry into professional courses at the undergraduate courses. The tests can be conducted every quarter. The students are free to take the test at their convenience. The entry into post-graduate level for the technology courses must be strictly through GATE or other similar entrance examinations. The curriculum should be reviewed and updated to be globally competitive. The teaching faculty should compulsorily attend programmes to update their knowledge and skills on the latest research and trends.

Consistency in quality amongst all technical education should be ensured. The role and powers of AICTE, MCI and other organisations responsible for accreditation needs to be merged into one single entity which would grant institutions an annual certification process based on the rating obtained from independent authorities. The institutions should explore methods of increasing their corpus and reduce their dependence on the Government for funding.

Establishment of Private Universities in the field of Science and technology should be encouraged. An enabling legislation for this purpose should be passed.

Adult Education

Issues

a. *Rapid Increase in Population*: The total population of the country has been increasing at a fast rate and is currently around one billion. Though, the literacy rate has also been consistently rising it has not been able to keep pace with the population growth rate. Consequently, the number of illiterates kept increasing for several decades. However, there has been a turnaround in the trend since 1991.

b. *Needed for a larger focus on certain states*: About one-third of the world's illiterates are in India. 48 % of the illiterates in India are in the four states of Bihar, Madhya Pradesh, Rajasthan and Uttar Pradesh.

c. *Functional literacy*: Concept of functional literacy and emphasis not on mere enrolment of learners but on attainment of certain predetermined norms and parameters of literacy, numeracy, functionality and awareness is not focussed.

d. *Rural-urban disparity*: The rural-urban disparity has posed a major problem with respect to literacy. However, in this decade the growth of literacy in the rural areas has been significant. In spite of the improvements in this decade the literacy percentage in the urban area is 80 % and in the rural areas is only 56 %.

e. *Economic disability*: Poverty is widely acknowledged to be the underlying cause for all the social problems facing India, illiteracy obviously being one of them. An individual in India, especially in the rural areas does not have the inclination towards education, since he would rather earn his living than spend time on getting educated. Hence the opportunity cost of learning is high. In other words, the utility from education is considered very low.

f. *Access*: Another critical reason to the slow growth of education could be attributed to access; in terms of time and place. The timings of the educational institutions/ communities are not convenient for most of the people. A common man will not compromise on his daytime to study since he has to sustain his family through employment. Also, the community centres imparting adult education are more concentrated in urban or semi-urban areas rather than rural areas. Basically, the reach of these programs is very poor and again it becomes inconvenient for a common man to access such education.

g. *Weak Policy Formulation*: A review of the efforts made so far in policy formulation and planning on training in adult education in India indicate that though meticulous planning has been done and concrete policy guidelines formulated but there is a lacuna in implementation of these programs and policies at the grassroots level. A number of research and evaluation studies have been conducted of the implementation of total literacy campaign (TLC) in India and these studies have revealed the following facts which need to be rectified immediately.

The weaknesses revealed by these studies are generally the following: -

— It is not primer specific.

— Lack of proper planning.

— Training needs are not properly identified.

— Appropriate training methods are not used (focus is on lecture method).

— Lack of relevant training materials on specific aspects of TLC.

— Proper monitoring, evaluation and documentation is not seen.

— Numbers of participants are bigger in size (un-manageable number)

— Insufficient support system for training.

— Same training model is followed in low and high literacy areas.

— Research in training is very poor.

— Development of training skills is not properly attended.

Imperatives for Sectoral Planning

India should achieve, by 2010 AD, 100 % literacy levels in the age group 6 to 65. The current estimates of NSSO state that by 2005, our literacy rate would be over 75 %. We would need support of a large number of organisations to achieve this, both within Government and outside of it. A comprehensive programme similar to those launched for polio vaccination needs to be organised involving large number of social organisations and NGOs. The responsibility should be placed with a single ministry who will co-ordinate with all the States and Union Territories for achieving the first objective.

Additional sources of funding for this programme should be explored. The norms for receipt of foreign funding for literacy programme to be liberalised. Focus should be more on the educationally backward states. Separate programmes for women illiteracy eradication, taking into account the social norms should be drawn up on a micro-management level.

5

ROLE OF RELIGIOUS INSTITUTIONS

India can boast an amazing cultural and religious diversity, though the Hindu tradition dominates everyday and festival culture. Some 80% of Indians are Hindus, about 11% Muslims, 2.4% Christians and 2.1% Sikhs; there are also Buddhists, Jainists and Parsees. Manifestations of cultural identity and religious customs are tightly interwoven into the fabric of daily public and private life, supporting the claim by orthodox Hindus that modern India is the legacy of a uniform Hindu tradition and not the product of cultural and religious diversity. At the same time, however, India is widely perceived by its inhabitants as the successful political model for a secular, tolerant, multiethnic state.

Government support for culture concentrates on a key area in the academies for literature, the fine arts, the performing arts, theatre, film and television, and on the major film festivals; traditional art forms are given support. The language situation in India is more complex than in virtually any other country in the world. As well as the two official languages, Hindi and English, a total of 17 regional languages are officially recognized.

The education system has been unable to keep up with population growth and reinforces existing social and regional disparities. Although the Indian Constitution provides for education for all, with school attendance compulsory, 57% of the Indian population is illiterate. The quality of education - from primary schools to universities - varies dramatically.

India has concluded cultural agreements with 102 states and agreed exchange programmes with 70 of them. Indian cultural institutes, the Tagore centres, have been set up in 12 countries (3 in Europe, in London, Moscow and Berlin). The Indian Council for Cultural Relations (ICCR), which is subordinate to the Foreign Ministry, organizes and finances numerous international cultural cooperation programmes and activities at home and abroad.

With the origins of Hinduism and Buddhism in India, religion is considered to be extremely important. Of the two religions, Hinduism is infinitely more popular, with an incredible 82 percent of the population practicing it. Within this majority, there are significant differences in the belief systems and caste divisions. Although there is division in some areas of Hinduism, there are many areas in common. They will all go to the pilgrimage sites, coming from all over India and will- if they go to a Brahman priest for birth, marriage and/or death rituals- hear the same Sanskrit verses from hundreds of years ago.

In the shadow of Hindu dominance, there are a few followers of other beliefs such as Christianity, Sikh and Buddhism. In India, religion is a way of life. It is an integral part of the entire Indian tradition. For the majority of Indians, religion permeates every aspect of life, from common-place daily chores to education and politics. Secular India is home to Hinduism, Islam, Christianity, Buddhism, Jainism, Sikhism and other innumerable religious traditions. Hinduism is the dominant faith, practiced by over 80% of the population. Besides Hindus, Muslims are the most prominent religious group and are an integral part of Indian society. In fact India has the second largest population of Muslims in the world after Indonesia.

Common practices have crept into most religious faiths in India and many of the festivals that mark each year with music, dance and feasting are shared by all communities. Each has its own pilgrimage sites, heroes, legends and even culinary specialties, mingling in a unique diversity that is the very pulse of society.

HINDUISM

The underlying tenets of Hinduism cannot be easily defined. There is no unique philosophy that forms the basis of the faith of the majority of India's population. Hinduism is perhaps the only religious tradition that is so diversified in its theoretical premises and practical expressions as to be called a "museum of religions". This religion cannot be traced to a specific founder nor does it have a "holy book" as a basic scriptural guide. The Rig Veda, Upanishads and the Bhagwad Gita can all be described as the sacred text of the Hindus.

Unlike most other religions, Hinduism does not advocate the worship of one particular deity. One may worship Shiva or Vishnu or Rama or Krishna or some other gods and goddesses or one may believe in the 'Supreme Spirit' or the 'Indestructible Soul' within each individual and still be called a good Hindu. This gives an indication of the kind of contrasts this religion is marked by. At one end of the scale, it is an exploration of the 'Ultimate Reality'; at the other end there are cults that worship spirits, trees and animals.

There are festivals and ceremonies associated not only with gods and goddesses but also with the sun, moon, planets, rivers, oceans, trees and animals. Some of the popular Hindu festivals are Deepawali, Holi, Dussehra, Ganesh Chaturthi, Pongal, Janamasthmi and Shiva Ratri. These innumerable festive occasions lend Hinduism its amazing popular appeal and make the Indian tradition rich and colorful.

Hindu Mythology

Heroes of epics like the Mahabharata and the Ramayana are immortalized and are still alive in the day-to-day existence of the common people. The gods of Hinduism are at once superhuman and human and there is distinct feeling of warmth and familiarity towards them.

Rama, the hero of the Ramayana, represents qualities such as honor, courage and valor and is held up as a model of manliness. His wife Sita is the prototypal Indian wife who is carried off by Ravana, the king of Lanka, while Rama and Sita are on exile. Sita's eventual rescue by Rama, his brother Lakshmana, and Rama's faithful monkey-general Hanuman are all woven into this engrossing tale. Stories from this epic have been passed down orally from one generation to the next. Religious fairs, festivals and rituals have kept these legends alive, and there is never an occasion that does not offer an opportunity to retell the old stories.

The stirring verses of the Mahabharata tell the story of the dynastic struggle between the Pandavas and the Kauravas, who were close cousins. Lord Krishna plays a very important role in this Great Epic. He is a friend, philosopher and guide to Arjuna, one of the Pandavas, and he helps Arjuna overcome his hesitation to kill his close relatives in the battlefield. The wise philosophy of Krishna and his teachings have been embodied in the Bhagwad Gita. Although the popular image of Krishna is that of a god who steals butter as a child, and who, as a youth, plays the flute and entices cows and cowherd girls alike; in his mature years he is depicted as the wise philosopher with a more serious side to his nature.

There are numerous gods and goddesses worshipped by Hindus all over India. Among these, the most fundamental to Hinduism, is the trinity of Brahma, Vishnu and Shiva - creator, preserver and destroyer respectively. Brahma has four heads corresponding to the four directions of the compass. He is the creator of life and the entire universe. Vishnu is the preserver who guides the cycle of birth and rebirth. He is also supposed to have taken many incarnations to save the world from evil forces. Both Rama and Krishna are believed to have been incarnations of Vishnu. Shiva, usually seen with a coiled cobra around his neck, destroys all evil and also has many incarnations, not all of which are terrifying.

The invisible deities are represented by a complexity of images and idols symbolizing divine powers. Many of these idols are housed within ornate temples of unparalleled beauty and grandeur. The Hindu gods are very much alive and live in temples, snow-capped peaks, in rivers and oceans and in the very hearts and minds of the Hindus.

Gurukul Education

Those who are fond of Gurukul education, know well its draw backs, but will not speak because of their vested interests. First thing gurukul was never open to the majority of masses. About 85 to 90 percent of population was outside the pale of Gurukuls. Only the 15 percent population was being catered by Gurukuls. That too, only the boys were admitted and not the girls, thus bringing the total possible population to be only about seven percent. There were no criteria for admission apart from the caste and whims and fancies of the teacher. Examples of denial of admission to very meritorious candidates on the basis of caste are seen.

Glaring example is of Eklavya. Not only the guru Dronacharya denied admission to Eklavya, but demanded Eklavya's thumb as gurudakshina for education NOT imparted by him. Many people feel it is irony of fate and mockery of awards, that such a name is associated with highest sports awards in this country, without any protest from the sufferers of the system. Second example is of Karna, who got admission to Parashurama's class, which was exclusively reserved for the Brahmins, on false statement of caste. Benefit of his knowledge, labeled as unlawfully obtained, was withdrawal when his caste became known, which ultimately lead to his death.

Example of Satyakama Jabala is mentioned by many orthodox people to erroneously show that education in Upanishadic times was open to low caste people. This is a wrong inference drawn from his story. Satyakama was asked by his guru his caste. His mother sent a word to the guru that she did not know the exact father of the child as she had relations with many people. This frank statement, the guru declared, can only be a statement of a son of a Brahmin. So the admission to the gurukul was done on the basis of Brahmin caste. Not only that, the test applied by him, and his presumption of Brahmin caste, was derogatory to non-Brahmins, because it was his belief that only Brahmins could speak such a truth and non-Brahmins could not have uttered such truth.

It may be noted that the declaration was made by the child's mother, who had no right to education. How a bold statement by mother can decide the caste of putative father, is a mystery, nobody has ever talked about. What were the criteria of selection of teachers in Gurukul? Propagators of Gurukul system seem to be very sure that teachers selected were of high caliber in knowledge and character. How this idea takes a root, is difficult to understand. As a matter of fact there was no central authority controlling the appointment of teachers. There was no fixed syllabus. The main purpose of this learning was to preserve the Vedas and guard them from non-Brahmins.

Each and every person by virtue of being born as a Brahmin had an inherent right to be a teacher. He could open an ashram and take pupils as and when he likes, and he could give certificate of completion of studies as and when he chooses. He was not bound by any law of land nor any convention of teachers' body. Most of the gurukuls were single teacher residential ones free from any royal or academic control. What was the guarantee of quality under these circumstances? It is a matter of egotism, vanity and conceit to think of quality in such teaching institutions. These gurukuls had no respect in foreign lands and never attracted any foreign students.

There seems to be misconceived idea that a student coming out from such a school had all the requisite qualities of a good citizen. This is far from the truth. He used to have learned by heart the Brahmanic sastras, which hardly make him versatile. He could never think of outside matters. What is not in his books, does not exist for him. Al Biruni, for example, mentioned that Indian scholars have no knowledge of civilization abroad, and they disbelieve if somebody tells them about it. Their thought process centered around the rituals, vratas and ceremonies. The Brahmanic knowledge consisted of recital of Vedas, without understanding the meaning of what is being recited, and was miles away from the actual life of productive castes.

As a matter of fact, it was enjoined that the reciter must not try to understand the meaning of what he reads. Prof. Kancha Ilaiah feels it ironical that "the recitation of several names of one God or many Gods is construed as wisdom, whereas knowing the language of production and the names of productive tools is not recognized as knowledge....". This system has remained in practice till this date and as a result of this todays education has suffered as he mentions: "... Because of their Vedic background, 'upper' castes perceive knowledge as reading and reciting. In the process they have rendered all higher educational institutions into text book recitation centres." He further observes:

> "The Dalitbahujan masses have enormous technological and engineering skills which are not divorced from their labour. One who lifts dead cattle also knows the science of skinning it. They themselves know how to process the skin and make chappals, shoes or ropes. All these tasks involve both mental and physical labour. This work is not like reading the Vedas or teaching in a school. Reading the Vedas or teaching in a school does not require much investment or physical labour or creative thought.... Why not celebrate the beauty and skill of a Gouda... Training in this specialization is much more dangerous and difficult than training in reading the Vedas....".

At one time even the Brahmins must have had the skill of skinning the animals, when, as Ambedkar puts it, "For the Brahmin every day was a beef-steak day". Ambedkar has discussed this topic in great detail with quotations from Atreya

Brahmana and concludes: "Brahmins were not merely beef-eaters but they were also butchers". But they lost this skill when they became vegetarians in order to outsmart the Buddhists. Therefore, during the days of decline of Buddhism, as a part of Kalivarjya changes in laws during the so called Rajput period, say from 900 - 1200 A.D., we find a restriction on the Brahmins, not to kill the animals themselves, and they were prohibited from becoming a "shyamitra", i.e. one who kills animals by strangling or suffocating, during a yajnya.

Ideals of Education in Brahmanism

The ideals of any system is depicted by the gods and goddess those are worshipped as depicting the ideal. Saraswati, as is well known, was originally a Buddhist deity as its earliest representation was evident in Buddhist monuments and not in Brahmanic ones. It was on Bharhut railing pillar, that there is a standing female figure playing on harp and J. N. Banerjea considers it as "the earliest representation of Saraswati in Indian Art." and that her separate figures became common from late Gupta period. Saraswati is depicted in late Brahmanism as the goddess of education by the Brahmins. As Kancha Ilaiah has explained, during the process of manipulating consciousness of Dalitbahujans to build consent systems among the groups they wanted to exploit, Brahmanism developed a socio-economic and cultural design systematically, so that many gods and goddesses of such groups, were adapted by Brahmanism creating images of many Gods against universal ethic of monotheism. Kancha Ilaiah further observes:

> "Brahma's wife is known as Saraswati, which also means learning. The construction of Brahma-Saraswathi relationship takes place strictly within the philosophical bounds of patriarchy. Brahma himself is shown as the source of wisdom in the Vedas, the early Brahmin writings, which were designed to subordinate the native masses of India. The Vedas themselves express the mixed feelings of crude Brahmanism. But since they were written by the

> Brahmins (i.e. by the early literate Aryans), the texts go against Dalitbahujans. In fact, they are anti-Dalitbahujan texts. The absurdity of Brahmin patriarchy is clear in these texts. The source of Education, Saraswati, did not write any book as the Brahmins never allowed women to write their texts. Nowhere does she speak even about the need to give education to women. How is it that the source of education is herself an illiterate woman? This is diabolism of the highest order. Brahmanism never allowed women to be educated. The first woman who worked to provide education for all women is Savitribai Phule, wife of Mahatma Phule, in the mid-nineteenth century. To our Dalitbahujan mind, there is no way in which Saraswati can be compared to Savitribai Phule. In Savitribai Phule, one finds real feminist assertion...."

He further observes:

> "... She (Saraswati) herself remains a tool in the hands of Brahma. She becomes delicate because Brahma wants her to be delicate. She is portrayed as an expert in the strictly defined female activities of serving Brahma or playing the veena - always to amuse Brahma. Brahma is never said to have looked after cattle, or driven a plough; similarly, Saraswathi never tends the crops, plants the seed or weeds the fields. She is said to have become so delicate that she could stand on a lotus flower. She could travel on a hansa (a swan, a delicate bird). This kind of delicateness is a negative delicateness. It only shows that her alienation from nature is total. In order to live this alienated but luxurious life, Brahmins have built up an oppressive culture. That oppressive culture was sought to be made universally acceptable.

After education, Brahmins main task involved in seeing that nobody transgress the caste rules, no widow gets remarried, see that all girls married before puberty, and generally nobody transgresses the caste. If anybody did transgress these rules, then this product of gurukul was to sit as the judge to punish the guilty by excommunication and ordeals and things like that, so that supremacy of Brahmin is maintained and the divinely ordained system of chaturvarna works smoothly to the advantage of some and peril to the rest.

If anybody has any doubt about the standard of education of gurukuls and has any wrong ideas, he better see what is recorded about the knowledge of Brahmins at time of Britishers' arrival. The Brahmins of Poona thought, their town was the whole world. They never tried to find out who were the British and from where they have come here. The believed that Calcutta was in England and England was in Calcutta. Any knowledge except Sanskrit was considered as a gate way to Hell. They honestly believed that Indra tells the cloud to pour down the rain. The clouds are the elephants of Indra and on his order they make rain. Poona was such a dark valley of ignorance. Such was the knowledge of scholars. The modern stories of intelligence of Birbal, Tenali Ram, and Nana Fadnavis are all fables, fabricated to stress upon the masses the false merit of Brahmin scholars over the royal princes.

Guru as God

It is true that Guru was elevated to the status of God. There are mantras chanted by Brahmins that guru is Brahma, guru is Vishnu, guru is Maheshvara, guru is real supreme godhead, to whom everybody must bow. So we find Brahma, Vishnu and Shiva, supreme divine trinity of post Vedic puranik gods to be of same status as guru. But that is not all. This mantra has to be remembered along with another sastrik injunction, that "Brahmin is the guru of all varnas" (varnanam brahmano guru). Brahmin saint Ramdas did not forget to mention this in Marathi also, guru to sakalancha brahman. A hindu is not supposed to take any instructions from anybody else other than Brahmin. This equates not the teacher with god but a Brahmin with god. And sure enough, they are called 'bhudevas' - gods on the earth.

If there were any prerequisites of such respect by the society for the gurus, like good conduct etc., then perhaps this could have been tolerable, but that is not so. That the Brahmin, even if becomes corrupt, he is still to be respected as supreme within the three worlds, as is pronounced by a Marathi Brahmin saint of seventeenth century, Saint Ramdas, in his religio-socio-political treatise - "Dasbodha". He also avers that Brahmin is guru of all; though he becomes inactive is still to be worshipped and that if an 'antyaja', (i.e. todays SCs, STs) becomes learned, still he is useless. At the time of Mahatma Jotirao Phule, his bitter critic was Vishnu Sastri Chipalunkar - the so called 'the Shivaji of Marathi language'. It is reported about him that, he thought country means not people, but its land, language, hindu traditions and history of famous people.

The pride of these was patriotism for him. His writings were miles away from reality and rationalism. He abused Phule by calling him 'shudra jagatguru', 'shudra poet', 'shudra dharma sansthapak' and said Phule 'barks' against Brahmins. He said Brahmins may be cunning and cruel, but one thing is sure, the keys of store house of knowledge are in their waist, and without these keys no other castes can be educated. He repeated old sastric injunction in an arrogant manner, that the world is under control of gods, the gods are under the control of mantras, and mantras are sole property of Brahmins, so Brahmins are the gods on earth.

During British times, some Europeans became College Professors and were teaching the Indian students, most, if not all, of them were Brahmins. This equation of gurus with god became quite intolerable to the Brahmins of the time, which made Shivaram Mahadev Paranjape, a learned Brahmin of Maharashtra, to pronounce that, 'he aamache guru ch navhet" - "these people are not our gurus at all". As explained above, since long, women are not allowed any education in Brahmanic system. Some scholars are at pains to tell us that, originally, women also took education. They point out the names of Maitereyi and Gargee in Vedic times. No doubt, there was a time, the sanskara of Upnayana was allowed to women. The more important point is when was it stopped and why.

Perhaps Manu Smriti could provide an answer, when it enjoined that women should be under care of father, husband or son and never independent. And also that the father who does not marry his daughter before age of eight, goes to hell. Why were these restrictions put? Just for weaning them away from Buddhism. On the contrary, women were educated in Buddhist centers till quite late. You can see a painting of about sixth or seventh century, in Ajanta, where a girl is sitting in front of a teacher along with boys.

When no teacher was available for Phule's school, Sawitribai got educated and became the first woman teacher in India after about two thousand years. Altekar tells us women teachers were not seen in India, since beginning of Christian Era. Today a woman can become a teacher, thanks to the British, but still she can not be a vedic teacher. Even in modern times a shankaracharya proclaims that women should not utter the vedic hymns. The reason he gave was not religious; perhaps he was too shy of giving a religious reason in this modern times. But the reason he gave was a biological one. He said that chanting of Vedic hymns would damage the female reproductive organs. Most astounding reason ever heard of. Medical fraternity of India is second biggest in the world, but nobody seems to have taken note of this new etiological factor in diseases of female anatomy, and commented on this. Very very scientific attitude indeed.

Creation of Illiteracy

Present India is illiterate, no doubt about it. But it was not so all the time. When Aryans were savages, there was an urban Dravidian civilization in India, the Harrapan Civilization, and they had their own script. Ashokan edicts are scattered all over India. They are written in Prakrit language, not in Sanskrit. It shows the language of people was Prakrit. As a matter of fact Sanskrit was not spoken anywhere, any time. It was an artificial language only meant for writing. Even in South India, the most ancient inscriptions are in Prakrit. Sanskrit inscriptions came later on. The mere presence of Ashokan Edicts denotes that Ashokan India was literate India. Historians believe that a great percentage of common people in Mauryan period were literate, who could read these edicts, which were meant for common people.

Otherwise, there was no sense in spending so much amount in inscribing the edicts and inscriptions on rock, pillar and caves. Dr. Vincent Smith is of the opinion that, "literacy in those days was higher than many provinces of the British regime." Nagesh Chaudhari, a prominent OBC scholar and editor of "Bahujan Sangharsha", on the authority of A. S. Altekar, mentions that the literacy rate during Ashoka's times was sixty percent. India is supposed to have largest number of illiterates in the world. Many institutions are fed on State revenue for the 'noble' cause of so called 'adult' literacy. But nobody tells us why India remained illiterate for centuries. It was Dr. Ambedkar who brought this fact in light. He averred that, without formal education the accumulated thought and experience relating to a subject can not learned by a student and he will not get new perception and his horizon will not widen. This requires schools, books and planned materials and literacy.

Formal education was confined study of to Vedas alone, in schools only for Brahmins, as they propagated that there was no knowledge outside Vedas. Education of rest was neglected by the state. Children of vaishyas learned rudiments of business geography and arithmetic from fathers in course of business, and so did the shudra craftsmen from their parents. This education was domestic and practical. Due to this illiteracy became inherent part of Hindus. Manu and others made laws to this effect. Those who had right to study the Vedas had right to read and write, others were deprived of this right. So according to laws of Manu, reading and writing has become the right of few high caste men and illiteracy has become the destiny of low caste multitudes. This is how literacy was prohibited and general ignorance prevailed among the masses. Such is the system of Gurukuls. It is very surprising and sad that, there are still in this age, some learned supporters of this system, which needs to be condemned out rightly.

The question arises, why there should be affinity in the minds of people for such gurukuls, which do not as a matter of fact exist today, except for a few attempts scattered in various states to revive Brahmanic schools, where English also is taught, so also modern archery but no science. Either it could be due to ignorance of exact nature of such gurukuls in the past and as a blanket glorification of everything that is ancient, or it may be a purposeful mischievous planed strategic tactic and a wily trick to promote Brahmin supremacy on the gullible 'masses' by the learned and knowledgeable 'classes'. The other reason could be the natural desire from nationalistic standpoint and thought that Brahmin culture of ancient India was the only culture available and we must glorify it, may be it was good or bad.

There is a feeling in the minds of many, that India is and was a Hindu country having always had a majority of Hindus. This again is a misconception. In historical times the population of India was never in majority of Hindus. Swami Vivekananda, estimated Buddhist to be two thirds of population and Dr. Ambedkar says Buddhist were in majority. Then there were Jains and Veerashaivas and Tribal religions in addition to Muslims, Sikhs and Christians. So taking Hinduism as religious faith, they were neither the most ancient nor the most numerous. If one considers Hindu not as religion but as geographical entity like as Hindu comes from pronunciation of Sindhu, then also one has to consider others as a part of, and rightful owners of, this land, irrespective of their religious faith. And Hindu or Aryan as cultural entity has a very poor claim and one could not accept the conditionality of respect for Rama and Krishna etc. as a precondition of nationality, as Gail Omvedt very rightly analyses the situation and comments:

"In other words, the construction of Hinduism as achieved by the Hindu-nationalists and accepted in various forms by many supposed secularists as well, rests on a trick: conflating the two contradictory definitions of a broad, territorial, pluralistic, historical identity with a religious culture that continues to give dominance to an Aryan / Vedic / Sanskritic / Brahmanic core."

Dr. Ambedkar very rightly said:

> "It must be recognized that there never has been a common Indian Culture, that historically there have been three Indias, Brahmanic India, Buddhist India and Hindu India, each with its own culture.... It must be recognized that the history of India before the Muslim invasions is the history of a mortal conflict between Brahmanism and Buddhism."

SIKHISM

The Sikh religion emerged during the early 16th century in the state of Punjab in North India. The founder of this faith was Guru Nanak, who from his childhood was attracted to both Hindu and Muslim saints. Born a Hindu, but also inspired by the teachings of Islam, he began to preach the message of unity of both religions. According to him, the basic teachings of both faiths were essentially the same. Nanak attracted many followers and came to be known as a Guru or a teacher. His disciples came together to form a new religious tradition called Sikhism.

The Gurus who followed Nanak contributed to the consolidation and spread of Sikhism. The teachings of Guru Nanak were incorporated in the 'Guru Granth Sahib', the Holy Book of the Sikhs which became a symbol of God for Sikhs. The fifth Guru, Guru Arjun built the Golden Temple at Amritsar which became the holiest of Sikh shrines. The tenth Guru, Govind Singh imparted military training to the Sikhs to help them defend themselves.

On Baisakhi day of 1699 at Anandpur, Guru Govind Singh ordered his Sikhs to assemble before him as was customary and created a new brotherhood of Sikhs called the Khalsa (Pure Ones). Five men selected for their devotion to the Guru were called Panj Pyares and given nectar (amrit) for initiation into the brotherhood of Khalsa. Later the Guru himself received initiation from Panj Payares as did others.

The members of the new brotherhood were instructed to wear the five symbols (the five Ks)- uncut hair, a comb, a steel wrist guard, a sword and breeches. The initiated men took the name Singh (Lion) and the women Kaur (Princess). The Guru also decided to terminate the succession of gurus and was thus the last of the Sikh Gurus.

Sikhism propounds monotheism, i.e. worship of one God. It also opposes the caste system and believes that all men are equal. However the ideas of karma and rebirth from Hinduism are accepted. Today, many Sikh practices are common to Hindus. Intermarriages between the two communities are also common. However the Sikh community has its own unmistakable identity. Though the Sikhs constitute less than 2 percent of the Indian population, they have become a distinct element in the configuration of the Indian religious tradition and the Indian society.

BUDDHISM

Buddhism originated as an offshoot of Hinduism in India, but eventually it became popular all over Asia. The personality and teachings of Gautam Buddha, the founder of this faith, have illumined the lives of millions of people in Japan, China and Southeast Asia.

There are strong lines of similarity between Buddhism and the basic teachings of Hinduism. Buddhism is based on the principle or the law of impermanence. According to this, everything is subject to change, although some things may last longer than others. The other basic principle of Buddhism is the law of causation, according to which nothing occurs due to pure chance. Besides natural forces, it is the karma which leads to the occurrence of all events. The popular notions of the indestructible soul and the cycle of rebirth emerge from these two basic philosophies.

Buddha advocated the Middle Path, in which he offered a balanced, harmonious way of life, steering between two extremes of self-indulgence and total abstinence. Buddhism rests upon four Noble Truths: (i) suffering is universal, (ii) it is caused by desire and yearning (iii) suffering can be prevented and overcome and (iv) eradication of desires can lead to removal of suffering. To prevent suffering one has to conquer craving and desire and this conquest leads to the attainment of nirvana or complete enlightenment.

Buddhist Educational System

This brings us to another question. What was the Educational system of Buddhists. Buddhists had their own educational system and was entirely based on different principles. Buddhists never believed in caste distinctions, they believed in equality of all men, they believed in equal status to women. Even during the decline of Buddhism, the education system continued through the Vajrayani Siddhas. The students used to utter 'om namao siddam' at the start of their studies. The present 'ganeshay namah' is quite recent. The remnant of this system of Siddhas, the word 'onama' meaning 'beginning' - a corrupted form of 'om namah siddham' - still exists in Marathi language.

To understand the difference between Brahmanic and Buddhist methods of education is a crucial point which should not be missed if one wants to realize the implications of the education system in Indian Society. The ancient India was known all over the world for Buddhist Education, not Brahmanic. Brahmanic education was essentially a single individual teacher with his small group of disciples and pupils at his residence. One teacher was teaching all the subjects, and there was no specialization. On the other hand, Buddhist system is institutional i.e. monastic. This difference is significant, leading to different lines of evolution. Prof. Mookerji says:

> "The necessity of a domestic environment in the Brahmanical system did not favour the expansion of a small school under an individual teacher into a large educational federation, controlled by a collective body of teachers, as was the characteristic of the Buddhist system."

It gave birth to those large scale monastic universities, with thousands of teachers and students, and attracted students from all over Asia. Evolution which continued for more than fifteen hundred years culminated in establishing Universities like Nalanda, Vallabhi, Vikramsila, Jagaddala, Odantpuri etc. Though these universities started as training grounds for monks, did not remain places for cloistered meditation but developed into seats of culture and learning and remained so till got destroyed by Muslim invasions. Those were the times, without any books, all teaching was imparted by word of mouth. Books came not before first century B.C. Students had to learn by heart Dhamma and Vinaya, and at the end of learning there used to be a ceremony of Paravarna, on the last day of varsavas.

The remnants of this Buddhist practice, remains even now in the form of "Kojagiri" in Maharashtra and by other names in other areas like "Pujagiri" in Bengal. During the course, there was unrestricted freedom to argue, to dispute, and debate and each was expected to think reason and decide for himself all matters of Vinaya and Dhamma, the facility, presumably was absent in gurukuls. The subjects were not only Dhamma and Vinaya but they were trained in e varied cultural subjects, in the tenets of other faith, in systems of philosophy, and even the subjects of pragmatic importance like Agriculture and Architecture. Afterwards, when books began to be written, these centers developed huge splendid manuscript libraries. We have seen in gurukuls, admission was based on basis of caste, reserved only to all dwijas technically, but only to Brahmins in practice, because in Kali yuga, there were only two varnas, Brahmins and Shudras, and the last Kshatriya kula was that of Nandas, because they did not want to recognize the Mauryas as Kshatriyas.

In Brahmanic Gurukuls, the course content differed according to caste of the pupil. In contrast, we also know that people of all castes were admitted to Buddhist Sangha, and in Buddhist centers of learning, the admission was open not only to monks of different Buddhist sects but, also to unordained seekers of knowledge and learning, even to non-Buddhists, irrespective of caste and sect, religious denomination or nationality. It is also worth noting that the system of education was totally free and for the benefit of residence and learning in a monastery, there could of course be no question of payment. The monasteries were maintained by grants from princes and people alike as an act of spiritual merit.

ISLAM

The Arab traders brought Islam to India in the early 8th century, but it was not until the 12th century that it became a force to reckon with in the Indian sub-continent. Unlike Buddhism, Jainism and Sikhism which emerged as offshoots of Hinduism, the concept, customs and religious practices of Islam were unique to this faith which professed universal brotherhood and submission to Allah - the God Almighty.

The Muslim invaders in the 12th century and the Mughal rulers in the 16th and 17th centuries helped in the spread of Islam in India. In its first phase, Islam was aggressive. But the mystics of Islam, or the Sufi saints, helped in spreading the message of peace and universal love.

The spirit of brotherhood propounded by Sufi saints and preachers like Kabir and Nanak helped in loosening the rigidity of the caste system. The interaction of the two faiths led to a synthesis of Hindu and Islamic elements in almost every sphere of life and culture. After an initial period of conflict and confrontation, today the two religions have accommodated and enriched each other.

CHRISTIANITY

Christianity first came to India by way of St. Thomas. He came to Kerala, in southwestern India, and founded the first church. Ironically, Shankaracharya, a Hindu reformer and seer, was born in Kerala some five hundred years after St. Thomas. St. Thomas ended up dying in the Chennai region (then known as Madras) of the Tamils.

Most Christians in India are Catholic (over 60 percent) and a majority of them are found in the south, particularly Kerala, Andhra Pradesh and Tamilnadu. Approximately on third of Kerala's population is comprised of Christians and they are involved in all aspects of society.

Contrary to popular belief, British rule had little to do with the growth of Christianity in India. The missionaries generally tended to turn public opinion, even those of the Indian Christians, against foreign rule. Bengali Christians in Calcultta were fairly important in their respective areas, whether it was in education, as a leader or an opinion-maker.

By tradition, Christianity is said to have arrived in India with Saint Thomas, one of the apostles of Jesus Christ, who spent some years in South India and possibly died there. However, others believe that the first missionary to arrive in the country was Saint Bartholomew. Historically, Christian missionary activity started with the advent of Saint Francis Xavier in 1544. He was followed by Portuguese missionaries at first and eventually by missionaries from other countries like Denmark, Holland, Germany and Great Britain. Throughout the 18th and 19th centuries Catholic as well as Protestant missionaries preached Christian doctrines in India and also made important contributions to social improvement and education in India.

Much of the modern influences in the Indian society can be attributed to the role of Christianity in India. Christian missionaries helped in setting up schools and colleges all over India and also spread the message of faith and goodwill in the country. Christianity and its teachings influenced a number of intellectuals and thinkers in India, including Mahatma Gandhi.

Today, the Christians in India number about 30 million and consist of people from every denomination of Christianity.

JAINISM

Jainism as a religious tradition was established in India about the same time as Buddhism. Mahavira, one of the jinas (conquerors) preached the Jain philosophy around the same time that Buddhism began.

Like Buddhism, Jainism rose against the corruption in the interpretation of Hinduism prevalent at the time. The underlying philosophy of Jainism is that renunciation of worldly desires and self-conquest leads to perfect wisdom. This faith believes in total abstinence and asceticism as practiced by the Jinas and the Tirthankars ("crossing-makers"). The "crossing refers to the passage from the material to the spiritual realm, from bondage to freedom. Followers of this faith accept the popular gods of Hinduism but they are placed lower than the jinas.

The focus of this religion has been purification of the soul by means of right conduct, right faith and right knowledge. This faith also enunciates complete non-violence and the Jain monks can be seen with their nose and mouth covered by a cloth mask to ensure that they do not kill any germs or insects while breathing. Today, Jainism has more than 3 million adherents in India and finds wide acceptance because of its philosophy of sympathy for all living beings.

ZOROASTRIANISM

The first Zoroastrians to enter India arrived on the Gujarati coast in the 10th century, soon after the Arabian conquest of Iran and by the 17th century, most of them had settled in Bombay. Zoroastrian practice is based on the responsibility of every man and woman to choose between good and evil, and to respect God's creations. The religion's founder, Zarathustra, who lived in Iran in 6000 BC was the first religious prophet to expound a dualistic philosophy, based on the opposing powers of good and evil.

Most Zoroastrians can be seen in Bombay today where they are known as Parsees. They have no distinctive dress and few houses of worship. Five daily prayers, usually hymns uttered by Zarathustra and standardized in the religious text Zenda Avesta, are said in the home or the temple, before a fire, which symbolizes the realm of truth, righteousness and order.

INDIAN MODERNIZATION: 1947 TO 1965

Both before and after the Republic of India became independent in July of 1947, Indian nationalists were concerned with enacting those reforms -- political, economic, cultural, even military—necessary for India to emerge from its impoverishment. The early years of independent India were marked by considerable disputes as to how this could be accomplished.

A large and vocal segment of the Indian political classes favoured the establishment of a planned economy, one that would divert India's financial resources towards the creation of a substantial base of heavy industry and a modern system of higher education, with the aims of creating a vanguard economic sector that could pull the rest of India's economy out of the Third World along with the necessary professionals and technicians.

Gandhi, for his part, drew upon the successes of the West's cooperatives, the pioneering development techniques of Yucatán, and his own personal preferences in the education and organization of India's illiterate and apathetic masses via community-level institutions. Were this development policy—what Gandhi and his supporters called sarvodaya, meaning "the uplift of all"—to be implemented, the priority would be given towards providing basic educational and medical services to the Indian masses and enforcing basic social and political rights for all people, with the aim of allowing India's hundreds of millions to provide a much larger population capable of participating in a modern economy. Following the dissolution of the Congress Party and the formation of the first Indian coalition government at the federal level in 1949, and the unfortunate death of Gandhi from natural causes in that year, sarvodaya policies were indeed adopted, with the sole exceptions being a complete rejection of the caste system and the financing of these programs not entirely through taxing of India's modern industries but with foreign loans and grants.

Though the Indian government continued to enforce national standards well into the 1960's, India's different states—from 1953, drawn strictly along linguistic lines, with Bombay being partitioned into Gujarat and Maharashtra, Hyderabad being absorbed for the most part into Andhra Pradesh, and so on—reacted to sarvodaya policies differently. At one end of the spectrum, the state governments and populations of the north Indian interior were quite hostile to these relatively egalitarian policies; the prominence of the upper castes in all aspects of life and the growth of exclusivistic Hindu nationalism made state governments very reluctant to countenance policies that would give members of lower castes, women, and non-Hindus an equal footing with conservatives, and accordingly sarvodaya was delayed as much as possible.

India's northwestern states —Haryana, Punjab, Delhi, and Himachal Pradesh—were more hospitable to the educational and medical elements of sarvodaya than the political and social elements, for fear of entirely disempowering historic hierarchies of power. The western states of Gujarat and Maharashtra, however, never mind the progressive southern states of Tamilnad, Karnataka, and especially Kerala; were exceptionally friendly to sarvodaya as a whole. The reasons for the openness of these five states to sarvodaya has been much debated, though most explanations concentrate upon the relatively high levels of industrialization and urbanization in these regions as well as their historic openness to trade and migration and the relatively low profile of conservative upper castes.

Regardless of the reasons, these five states went to great lengths to enforce sarvodaya: state governments did at least try to ensure civil and political equality for all of their citizens, affording even Muslims relative freedom from persecution, while state governments did go to considerable expense, even drawing heavily upon state budgets, to establish dense networks of primary schools and medical centres for the largest segments of their populations.

The progress acheived by sarvodaya was slow, at first, but as the 1950's ended and the 1960's began signs of progress began to appear. For instance, thanks to the new networks of schools and medical centres, literacy rates rose sharply even as death rates dropped by some 30% between 1951 and 1961 as reported by successive national censuses, and these improvements could be directly correlated to the relative enthusiasm of each state in adopting sarvodaya. In the five western and southern states, one unexpected result was an above-average decrease in birth rates, traceable to the better health and education of these populations as well as to the beginnings of female empowerment.

In Kerala, sarvodaya was augmented by the formation of financial cooperatives by peasants and the urban poor. Inspired by European models and organized by indigenous democratic Communists, Kerala's financial cooperatives played a preeminent role in providing non-traditional entrepreneurs—peasants, for instance, or women—with the capital needed to create their own businesses. Before long, the "Keralan model" was being copied throughout India.

Simultaneously, the "Bombay Plan" proposed by economists C.N. Vakil and P.R. Brahmanand suggested that capital-poor India could develop quickly by exploiting its very large workforce to produce "wage goods," simple consumer products like clothes, toys, radios, and bicycles. These low-capital low-risk manufacturing processes would attrack domestic and foreign investment even as they enhanced the consuming power of the masses and pushed investments into agriculture and rural infrastructure. This plan was controversial for its neglect of heavy industry, and it was never implemented fully. Inasmuch as it was implemented, though, it worked quite well with the principles of sarvodaya. Within a short time after the partial adoption of the Bombay Plan's principles, industrial growth began to accelerate in northwestern India.

The Second Indo-Pakistani War of 1965 coincided with the Indian federal government's White ·Paper of National Development. This government document reviewed the successes achieved by sarvodaya nation-wide and in selected states and concluded that with almost half of the Indian population possessing basic literacy skills and life expectancies estimated to be as high as an estimated 55 years, and with the enfranchisement of broad swathes of the Indian population, India's newly large and relatively healthy and educated population could well trigger rapid economic growth like that experienced elsewhere in the Third World.

India's hard-fought military victory over Pakistan signalled the beginning of a shift in state and federal government policies, as increasing amounts of government (and private) funds were shifted into higher education and heavy industry, while foreign investors began to establish off-shore manufacturing plants in the KeKaTMaGu states. Nonetheless, the basic policies of sarvodaya remained in effect throughout India until the Third World War and the end of the Indian state in 1982, and were enthusiastically copied throughout the Third World.

MEDIA EDUCATION

Generally speaking, media education in India is still in an experimental stage and the feedback it receives from within the country or continent is very little, as most of the conferences take place in Europe. Another reason for this lack of progress is the fact that the concepts of media education are rather geared to the Western hemisphere.

India is a third-world country and therefore the aims it pursuits in media education are different from those in Europe. For India, the emphasis is rather on development and liberation. Kumar believes that media education should lead to democratic communication, while he refers his concepts of media education to all third-world countries.

In India, there is a clear distinction between the term media education, which describes education aiming at a critical use of media; the term educational technology , which, apart from conveying all teaching techniques, also includes the use of media in school lessons; and the term professional education in the media, which can be regarded as a mixture of a school of journalism and of film.

Keval Kumar´s definition of media education could therefore be understood as a teaching method that uses formal, non-formal, and informal approaches to impart a critical understanding of various media in order to lead to greater responsibility, greater participation in the production of media as well as to a greater interest in the sales and reception of media.

According to Kumar, a major aim of media education is making the media more accessible to society (he is thinking less of individuals here), so that they can be used more efficiently for public interest and welfare instead of being simply useful for the producer´s profit. It is regarded as equally important, however, to raise and convey critical awareness, as this enables people to intervene actively in the production process instead of simply passively consuming media.

A further aim is to make this awareness usable in a democratic sense. On the whole, media education in India is aiming at enlightening the masses against despotism as well as it is supporting the liberation from the status of a third-world country. Television and cinema ca be employed for `enlightening´ as it is also accessible for the illiterate. Kumar rightly assumes that uneducated consumers of the media also reflect upon them instead of simply being manipulated by them, as is generally argued.

There is a distinction between media education and educational technology. Media Education is learning about media and educational technology is learning by using media. The latter is integrated into the curriculum of the Indian teacher training institutes (schools of education) to enable teachers to make use of media in their lessons.

Learning about media does not take place within the institute, but is promoted by individual persons or by religious institutions as non-formal activities. These religious, social or political groups that employ media education, do so in order to point to its manipulatory or morally destructivecharacter or even for their own undemocratic (and also democratic) aims. Kumar does not object to this political side, even deems it necessary as long as it helps to improve public welfare, i.e. for social purposes or to remedy any grievances. In practice, however, pure textual criticism is still more popular than elucidation.

In the south of India, there are some media educationists employed in several church schools, in the Department of Communication as well as in some non-government organisations. Professional groups working in this field include church officials, teachers, university teachers and social workers.

Media Education in India is being obstructed by two things: On the one hand, the education system is only brought into line with the exams for which it prepares; on the other hand, there are the curricula which are centrally controlled by the government, so that media education depends on government policy.

Kumar identifies another problem in media education itself.It should be taught as a cross-curricular theme, as a subject `media education´ would overvalue the media and separate it from its social context. This over-evaluation would then again lead to a theory of manipulation. As a separate subject, media education should only be offered in Further Education.

Media Education finds no mentioning in the Curricular and it cannot be perceived that it will in the near future. There are classes dealing with the use of media (educational technology) , but none dealing with media education as learning about media. Occasionally, there are seminars and conferences on the topic, but most of the time the media educationist works individually, which is not a surprise in a large country almost as large as a continent

The frequent irrationality of the media, which in India are being controlled almost exclusively by political or commercial interests, nearly call for media education and this is why Keval Kumar ascribes great relevance to it. In India, there is a rise in fundamentalism and nationalism connected with an increasing industrialisation and with only a mall number of people profiting from (f.e. the software industries).

Media education is therefore being regarded as a device against despotism. According to Kumar there is only very little literature on this topic available. However, there are two video tapes introducing the topic of media education

Television and radio

Up to 90% of the Indian population can be reached by the state-owned television network Doordarshan via the terrestrial broadcasting system, and over 98% by the state-owned radio network All India Radio. Up until 1991 Doordarshan had a monopoly, but since then satellite TV has been allowed, originally only via cable networks. The audience shares of private cable news stations (Star TV/NDTV and CNBC in English, TV Today and Eenadu TV in Hindi) are continually increasing in the country's dynamic media market. These broadcasters primarily reach urban elites and help shape opinion. Several private broadcasters are planning additional English news channels from mid-2003.

Print media

India has a lively, critical, open, quality press. English-language dailies account for 17% of total newspaper sales, Hindi papers for 36%, and the rest is taken up by papers in several dozen regional languages. 5,638 different daily papers have a total daily print run of just under 60 million. Three of the four largest dailies are in English: The Times of India (2.15 million), The Hindu (937,000), The Hindustan Times (909,000). The main weekly periodicals are India Today (970,000) and Outlook (400,000).

The Indian press is predominantly in the hands of major Indian industrialists. In a very controversial decision on principle at the end of June 2002, the Indian government decided to open up the print media to foreign investment. In future, foreigners will be able to own up to 26% of publications containing news and daily events, up to 74% of scientific and other specialist publications. The first decrees necessary to implement this cabinet decision were issued in December 2002.

SPIRITUAL INSTITUTIONS AND ITS FUNCTIONS

The spiritual institution is a place of training for suitably equipped temperaments and mature minds towards the acquisition of the higher knowledge of human life. This specialised knowledge is not like one of the sciences or the arts taught in modern colleges or universities, among which a student can prefer anyone to the exclusion of others, but it is the central art and science which enables one to recognise the true meaning of life in general.

Spiritual life is not one of the ways of living or even one of the stages of life, but that general background of motive and understanding which vitalises all stages and gives life and meaning to every way of thinking and mode of activity. One cannot live wisely and successfully in the world without adopting the spiritual perspective of the Universe.

Spirituality is not worship of the deity in a temple, performance of rituals, following any code of behaviour or conduct, or even the practice of any cult, creed or religion. It is not even faith in God merely, for it rises above even this concept. Spirituality is that comprehensive understanding and envisagement of values, by which the Universe is taken in its totality-not in bits or parts-by which its unity is recognised. Not merely this; the aim of spiritual life is the recognition and realisation of this totality of the Universe as a single omnipresent, omniscient and omnipotent Self, or Atman. Obviously, this is a solution to all human ills, and all problems in creation.

The spiritual philosophy makes one the best of any kind,- a farmer becomes the best farmer, a gardener the best gardener, a driver the best driver, a clerk the best clerk, an official the best official, a teacher the best teacher, and so on. The noblest element in a person is brought out by the technique of spiritual living. It is, thus, not a question of option left to people or a theme to be discussed as to whether it is necessary or unnecessary, for it is the only meaning of all existence. The Institutions that teach this science and art of life are the spiritual organisations of the world and their existence is naturally a 'must' for the benefit and the peace, plenty and prosperity of mankind.

Anyone devoted to the ideals of truth, non-violence and purity can become a member of the Divine Life Society which is a non-sectarian Institution, embodying in its wide perspective the common fundamental principles of all the religions of the world, and of spiritual life in general. The Society accords equal place of honour to all faiths and religious traditions, and its members recognise no distinction or disruptive sentiment on account of each other's different traditional background, or religious affiliation, all which the principles and the philosophy and teachings of the Society do integrate.

Sri Swami Sivananda's profound teachings that each soul is potentially divine and that everyone's goal is to strive to manifest this divinity within by controlling the internal and external nature by 'being good and doing good'. Anyone with the above ideals is welcome to become a member of the Divine Life Society. The Divine Life Society has been a pioneer in advocating and popularising health, culture and physical fitness through daily practice of yoga asanas and surya-namaskara among the students and youth of India. This health-building work it has been doing through the length and breadth of India, from Rishikesh to Kanyakumari, and from Assam to the Punjab, since the past about forty years.

The Founder Swami Sivanandaji Maharaj had commenced this valuable yoga work even before. His world-wide yoga practice movement was one of the earliest movements in this direction. The organisation and spiritual work of this Society being entirely non-sectarian, non-denominational and fully tolerant in its nature, it has been a cementing factor amongst the people of this country. The Ashram has drawn its residents from all provinces in India. Its Branch Centres are to be found throughout the country and their spiritual work fosters tolerance and encourages national unity.

The Institution propagates unity of religions and goodwill among the communities. Almost all its annual Conferences, at State level as well as All-India level, feature one or two sessions as All-Religions-Meet or Sarva-Dharma-Sammelana. Thus, its work is intended to function as a constructive force promoting goodwill and harmony and peaceful relationship in India's society. This Society's spiritual teachers in foreign countries have been welcomed everywhere as the country's cultural and spiritual ambassadors of goodwill, who have endeared themselves to countless people by their sincerity and their service in the field of yoga.

The vast goodwill thus earned for India and its spiritual science (adhyatma-vidya) is an invisible and yet a tangible asset whose value cannot be easily estimated. This good work is spreading progressively all over the world. Even long before any of our present-day teachers had started to go abroad, Swami Sivananda's spiritual teachings and yoga literature had made such a powerful impact in other countries during this recent era that it had raised the name and the prestige of our nation and its culture to very great heights in the eyes of the educated peoples of numerous foreign countries the world over.

His books on yoga were very eagerly translated into French, German, Latvian, Estonian, Italian, Danish and Spanish languages, with the earnest objective of bringing about the widest possible spread of our country's most precious spiritual heritage. The dignity and eagerness of the country's cultural heritage has obviously risen high in the eyes of the peoples of other nations by this Institution's work.

A perusal of the spiritual teachings and a careful examination of the work of the Institution can make it evident that it has been propagating practices and indirectly working for targets for which the Government itself is now working and striving through various means and methods. Aims and goals such as national health and physical fitness, integrity of character, dutifulness and discipline, avoidance of wastage, limitation of family size, simplicity and thrift have been directly propagated and taught to people by this Institution from the time of its most revered Founder, who was known throughout India as one of the foremost spiritual leaders of his time and an illustrious well-wisher of the country, its people and its culture.

About a hundred or more deserving students of Uttar Pradesh, most of them from the very poor and backward District of Tehri-Garhwal, are receiving regular educational aid from the Institution for their school and college studies. In addition to their fees, the Institution helps them for their text-books as well as for their school uniforms and clothes. Besides this, the Ashram sometimes gives aid to poor and deserving schools nearby to help them out of their monetary problems and difficulties.

On the health and medical side, the Society, besides its regular year-round free medical service rendered to the public through the Ashram's Hospital, has conducted (a) twenty Eye Camps for free surgical and medical treatment of the public; (b) twenty Annual Women and Children's Medical Treatment Camps; (c) three First Aid Training Courses; and (d) a few Child and Maternity Welfare (prenatal) Camps and food and nutrition education exhibitions. Such medical relief and service activities are carried on by a number of its Branches in different parts of India.

The Divine Life Society has reclaimed from the streets a large number of leper beggars and is providing for their maintenance in their own settlements. These leprosy patients have thus stopped begging on the streets since some years past and improved their general health. Medical care is provided to them. Also periodical repairs to their hutments and supply of clothes are made to them. In addition to this humanitarian Social Welfare project, the Society also bears a major part of the financial burden of running another leprosy colony of more than 120 leprosy patients since the past many years.

The Institution has been a regular and unfailing participator in a number of national schemes by contributing appreciably towards Small Savings Fund, National Savings Certificates, Defence Bonds and collection drives undertaken by the Government. It also contributes its share in times of natural calamities like famines, epidemics, floods, etc. As a centre of revival, propagating and perpetuating the country's invaluable cultural heritage, the Institution's yeoman service is very well known throughout this nation over the past three decades.

The Headquarters Ashram has ever tried to be a haven of refuge for persons in distress, disappointment, grief, dejection, friendlessness and despair. The grieving and the sorrowful, the agitated and the confused come here for peace and solace. Such people rest and recover in this place and return in a better condition to face their problems and situations. No distressed person is ever turned away without assistance. No hungry person is ever refused a meal at the Ashram's kitchen. No shelterless person is ever turned away without night's shelter here. Through the years men and women, old and young, high and low, all come to this Institution on the banks of the Ganga by the highway to the Himalayan shrines, seeking to fulfil some inner want, some indefinable need.

In the name of the Almighty, the Institution strives to fulfil in some measure the inner need of countless persons. The value and importance to their lives of what they find and receive here is only known to them and can be assessed only by them. The Divine Life Society has been not only helping and supporting the imparting of education by normal schooling but also imparting education by correspondence. The Society is conducting classes on yoga, vedanta and Indian Culture in general, including classes in Sanskrit language, music, physical culture etc., regularly, throughout the year.

Postal correspondence work is also done on spiritual and cultural subjects, as well as themes of humanitarian service. Further, at periodical intervals, trained instructors from our Society are invited by the National Academy of Administration in Mussoorie and the Officers Training School, Nainital, to give training in yoga for the benefit of the officer trainees of the Academy. Thus, I.A.S. Probationers attending the foundational course as well as senior officers attending Advance Management Development and Planning course conducted at the National Academy of Administration have undergone training under the able Instructors deputed by the Society. Similar such training courses are conducted in different parts of the country in places like factories, industrial townships, universities like the Pantnagar University, the Delhi University, the Jawaharlal Nehru University, New Delhi, etc.

The aim of the Yoga-Vedanta Forest Academy of this Society is not merely an academic equipment of students, but a providing of the requisite training to enable them in their endeavour to blossom into truly humane, serviceful, integrated personalities, so that they succeed, at least in an appreciable measure, in living a life of goodness and wholeness personally, and of dedication, unselfish cooperation and constructive work socially. It needs no special mention that this achievement in one's own person and in society is obviously rooted in the extent to which one's practical life is attuned to the Ultimate Reality of the Universe.

Philosophical discipline, thus, is the pre-condition to leading a perfectly sociable, ethical and progressive life of an onward expansion towards the realisation of the Supreme Goal of existence. The teachers of the Academy will strive to hold aloft this objective set before the students, and are not just instructors in the well-known intellectual sciences. The basic spiritual foundation of all life is the principal motive governing the curriculum of the Academy, and students with this elevated spirit of quest seek admission.

Every year the Society also conducts intensive training camps in which people from all walks of life from every region, irrespective of caste, colour or creed, take part. During this period intensive training on yogasanas, pranayama and meditation is given to the participants. During the morning and evening sessions, instructive and illuminating discourses on the theory and practice of leading a spiritual life with a view to develop the integrated personality of man even while attending to the normal duties in one's respective walks in life are given.

In India, as in other parts of the world, all true charitable activities are carried on with a spiritual zeal which oversteps the boundaries of classes, creeds and cults. The Divine Life Society is religious if by religion we are to understand the grounding of one's life in the structure of a Cosmic Reality. But, no one, definitely, we hope, would be prepared to abrogate the need for such a religion, if religion is the name we prefer to give to it. It is, rather, the Science of Life, on whose basis this Society has always been working ever since its inception. It attempts to make man human to enable him to live at peace with himself and the Society at large. It lays emphasis on the brotherhood of man to regulate his conduct with his fellow beings and to promote a sense of unity among things.

The Divine Life Society is essentially a Charitable Institution and its main object is education, spread of knowledge, promotion of cultural progress, medical relief and relief of the poor. The fact that the workers engaged in carrying out the objectives of the Society have faith in a Super-Power that guides the destinies of men and believe that the ultimate goal of human endeavour should be to realise and experience oneness with that Power, would only adumbrate the integral approach of the Society as a whole.

Religion, to the Divine Life Society, does not mean any particular faith, creed or cult, or any 'ism' in the sense it is usually construed with relevance to the organised, the traditional or the accepted religions of the world. To this Institution, and to all its followers, religion means that consciousness or that conduct which manifests in practical life as well as personal demeanour the laws that are supposed to operate behind the working system of the universe.

Thus, religion becomes a scientific principle, a philosophical necessity and a spiritual ideal which regulates human life in every field of its activity,-personal, social, national or international. Thus, again, religion becomes an inviolable law of the world as a whole, by which individuals are united into a fraternity or brotherhood in the light of a total culture of humanity which may be said to be directed towards the achievement of the purpose of human life as such, without any distinction characteristic of the ordinary religions. This feature exemplifies the 'universal nature' of the activities and the aims and objects of the Society.

The Yoga-Vedanta Forest Academy trains seekers in the knowledge of India's Culture and in the practice of Yoga as a general discipline for developing integral personality as well as human welfare.

The Educational Activities of the Society consist in helping poor and deserving students, about a thousand in number right from the primary standard to the post-graduate level, by providing them free with the requisite facilities in their studies, as a gesture of the Ashram's goodwill towards the welfare of people. The Leprosy Relief Work of the Society is so well-known that it has always been regarded as part and parcel of the love extended by the Society to some 200 or more leper-patients who are rehabilitated and taken care of in a suitable manner. The Social Service Wing attends to such services as medical aid to the poor and needy, contribution towards different relief works in the country, and such other gestures of charity as would relieve the sufferings of people, in some measure, from poverty, disease and ignorance.

The fundamental aims and objects of the Divine Life Society, as a whole, are purely spiritual, entirely non-sectarian, universally applicable and perfectly tolerant. The Society offers a peaceful haven wherein is provided ample opportunity and actual help for the restoration of peace to the troubled, conflict-ridden and psychologically traumatised personality of the modern man.

Aims and Objects

I. To Disseminate Spiritual Knowledge

(a) By publication of books, pamphlets and magazines dealing with ancient, oriental and occidental philosophy, religion and medicine in the modern scientific manner, and their distribution on such terms as may appear expedient to the Board of Trustees;

(b) By propagating the Name of the Lord, and by holding and arranging spiritual discourses and conferences and frequent Sankirtans (singing the Lords name) or spiritual gathering for singing and glorifying the Name of the Lord;

(c) By establishing training centres or societies for the practice of Yoga, for moral and spiritual Sadhanas (spiritual practices) and the revival of true culture, to enable aspirants to achieve regeneration through worship, devotion, wisdom, right action and higher meditation with systematic training in asanas (postures), pranayama (breathing exercise), dharana (concentration), dhyana (meditation) and samadhi (superconscious state); and

(d) By doing all such acts and things as may be necessary and conducive to the moral, spiritual and cultural uplift of mankind in general and to the attainment of the above-mentioned objects in Bharatavarsha(India) in particular;

II. To Establish and Run Educational Institutions

On modern lines and on right basic principles and to help deserving students by granting them refundable and non-refundable scholarships for doing research work in the various branches of existing scriptures and comparative religion, as also to train them to disseminate spiritual knowledge in the most effective manner.

III. To Help Deserving Orphans and Destitutes

By rendering them such assistance as the Society may deem proper, whether in any individual case or in any particular class of cases;

IV. To establish and Run Medical Organizations

Or any other medical institutions and hospitals or dispensaries for the treatment of diseases and dispensing medicines and performing surgical operations, etc., to the poor in particular and to the other public in general, on such terms and in such manner as may be deemed expedient by the Board of Trustee.

PRESENT SITUATION OF EDUCATION

A few words about present situation may not be out of place. There is total negligence towards Primary Education. Even where the Rulers are OBCs, they are so much under the mental Slavery of Brahmanism, that as one OBC scholar puts it, they have the Brahmanic head over their trunk. There is a notable exception of Laloo Prasad Yadav, the Chief Minister of Bihar, who is highly maligned by media. He introduced what are known as "Charavaha Schools", the "cowherds schools", where teachers are sent to the cattle grazing grounds and teach the boys tending the cattle there.

Brahmanic media has not focussed enough attention on these attempts of new and revolutionary approach. When, this year, the Government of Maharashtra introduced English as one of the subjects from Class I, in Primary schools, there was a hue and cry in Brahmanic Press, being afraid of coming competition from these municipal schools products in future. As a matter of fact, the time has come, in spite of total Brahmanical opposition, to introduce English as a medium of Instruction right from Pre-Primary classes upto the highest level. The regional language medium should be stopped immediately and replaced by English. It would help lower strata of society, and encourage national integration. Recommendations made by Mahatma Phule to Hunter's Education Commission in 1882, are relevant still today. He emphasized the need for education to be compulsory and free, at least, upto 12 years of age for all castes. He had recommended more funds for Primary education for backward castes rather than higher education to upper castes. He demanded the higher education be brought within the reach of poor classes, and books be published as Govt. Gazettes.

6

EDUCATION AS AN AGENT OF SOCIAL CHANGE

HUMAN RIGHTS EDUCATION AND CURRICULUM DEVELOPMENT

Human rights are the result of humanity's increasing and persistent demand for dignity, respect, justice, protection and freedom-all needed for a decent human existence. The contemporary conception of human rights has historical roots. Rousseau, Socrates, and Plato in the West, and Manu, Vyasadeva, Gandhi, Aurobindo, and others in India have enunciated principles of human rights. Important milestones in the struggle for human rights are the struggle between the British crown and Parliament, the French revolution, the struggle for American independence, the Russian revolution, and the adoption of the Universal Declaration of Human Rights by the United Nations on 10 December 1948.

The Declaration symbolized the beginning of the international human rights movement. In 1959, children's rights to life, education, health, protection, and development were proclaimed in the Declaration of the Rights of the Child. The Universal Declaration of Human Rights embodies a set of guarantees enabling one:

— not just to live but to live with dignity;

— to develop fully and use one's human qualities, intelligence, talents, and conscience; and

— to satisfy one's physical, mental, social, and spiritual needs.

In other words, it asserts one's right to be human. The first sentence of the Declaration states that respect for human rights is the "foundation of freedom, justice and peace in the world." The Declaration has influenced the constitutions and legal systems of various countries. It was followed by many other declarations issued at the International Congress on Human Rights, the International Congress on the Teaching of Human Rights organized by UNESCO, the Seminar on the Teaching of Human Rights, and the United Nations World Conference on Human Rights, which recommended the adoption of the United Nations Decade for Human Rights Education.

The past half-century since the adoption of the UN Charter has been dismal for human rights. Some have called it catastrophic. Human rights education is stressed in all human rights documents as "an essential contribution to the development of a global human rights culture." It is universally accepted that education is the best source of social mobility, equality, and empowerment, both at the individual and collective levels. Further, it is considered as a precondition for a healthy democratic society. It is thus important that education include the study of peace, human rights, and democracy as essential to society's development.

The Declaration states the following: Every one has the right to education. Education shall be free at least at the elementary and fundamental stages. Elementary education shall be made generally available and higher education shall be equally accessible to all on the basis of merit.

Education shall be directed to the full development of human personality and to the strengthening of respect for human rights and fundamental freedoms. It shall promote understanding, tolerance, and friendship among all nations, racial or religious groups and further the activities for maintenance of peace. The International Covenant on Economic, Social and Cultural Rights reaffirms and strengthens these provisions. The 1978 International Congress on the Teaching of Human Rights and the 1993 Vienna conference called upon UN member-states to introduce human rights education at all levels of education.

The World Congress on Human Rights in Delhi, 1990, urged that human rights education be understood as encompassing formal, nonformal, and informal education systems, and also reach parents and policymakers. It aimed to develop awareness of how to translate human rights into social and political reality. The 1993 Vienna conference reiterated the urgency of respecting human rights and fundamental freedoms, and emphasized that human rights education must be treated as essential to the development of a global human rights culture. Four paragraphs of the Vienna Declaration and Programme of Action are related to education and training:

The World Conference on Human Rights considers human rights education, training and public information essential for the promotion and achievement of stable and harmonious relations among communities and for fostering mutual understanding, tolerance and peace. States should strive to eradicate illiteracy and should direct education towards the full development of the human personality and to the strengthening of respect for human rights and fundamental freedoms. The World Conference on Human Rights calls on all States and institutions to include human rights, humanitarian law, democracy and rule of law as subjects in the curricula of all learning institutions in formal and non-formal settings.

Human rights education should include peace, democracy, development and social justice, as set forth in international and regional human rights instruments, in order to achieve common understanding and awareness with a view to strengthening universal commitment to human rights. Taking into account the

World Plan of Action on Education for Human Rights and Democracy, adopted in March 1993 by the International Congress on Education for Human Rights and Democracy of the United Nations Educational, Scientific and Cultural Organization, and other human rights instruments, the World Conference on Human Rights recommends that States develop specific programmes and strategies for ensuring the widest human rights education and the dissemination of public information, taking particular account of the human rights needs of women.

Pursuant to the Vienna Declaration, the UN declared 1995-2004 as the United Nations Decade for Human Rights Education. The Decade's Plan of Actions aims to accomplish the following:

— Assess needs and formulate strategies to further human rights education at all school levels, in vocational training and formal as well as nonformal learning.

— Build and strengthen programs and capacities for human rights education at the international, regional, national, and local levels.

— Coordinate the development of human rights education materials.

— Strengthen the role and capacity of the mass media in the furtherance of human rights education.

— Globally disseminate the Declaration in the most number of languages possible and in other forms appropriate for various levels of literacy and for the disabled.

Human rights education is defined as training, dissemination, and information efforts aimed at building a universal culture of human rights by imparting knowledge and skills, and molding attitudes. Human rights education has five dimensions:

— strengthening respect for the human personality and its dignity;

- — fully developing the human personality and its dignity;
- — promoting understanding, tolerance, gender equality, and friendship among all nations, indigenous peoples, and racial, national, ethnic, religious, and linguistic groups;
- — enabling all persons to participate effectively in a free society; and
- — furthering the activities of the United Nations to maintain peace (Guidelines for national plans of action for human rights education-UN-A/52/469/Add.1.)

THE INDIAN CONSTITUTION AND HUMAN RIGHTS

The Constitution shapes the country's concept of human rights. The Preamble, Fundamental Rights, Fundamental Duties, and Directive Principles of the State policy are concrete steps toward the realization of human rights. Whereas basic objectives have been defined in the Preamble, the protection of human freedom and liberties are emphasized in Fundamental Rights and Directive Principles of State Policy. The rights of the child have been given the greatest priority. Since rights and duties are inseparable, Fundamental Duties are also imperative. These provisions epitomize the collective will and aspiration of all Indians. The following provisions in Constitution safeguard human rights:

- — equality before the law (Article 14);
- — nondiscrimination on ground of religion, race, caste, sex, and place of birth (Article 15);
- — equality of opportunity (Article 16);
- — freedom of speech, expression, assembly, association, movement, residence, acquisition, and disposition of property, practice of any profession, carrying out any occupation, trade, or business (Article 19);
- — prohibition of traffic in human beings and forced labor (Article 23);

- prohibition of labor in case of children below 14 years (Article 24);
- freedom of religion (Article 25);
- no provision for religious instruction in any educational institution wholly maintained out of State funds (Article 28);
- conservation of language, scripts, and culture (Article 29 [1]);
- right of minorities to administer educational institutions (Article 30);
- State guarantee of social order (Article 38 [1], Directive Principles of State Policy);
- adequate means of livelihood, equal pay for equal work for both men and women, non-abuse of health of the worker, opportunity for children to develop in a healthy manner and in conditions of freedom and dignity (Article 39, Directive Principles of State Policy);
- right to work, education, and public assistance in specific cases (Article 41, Directive Principles of State Policy);
- provision for free and compulsory education of children up to 14 years of age (Article 45, Directive Principles of State Policy); and
- ensuring education and economic development of scheduled castes, scheduled tribes, and other weaker sections of society (Article 46, Directive Principles of State Policy).

Educational Policies and Human Rights

The reports of various Education Commissions and the statement of educational policy have articulated the importance of the right to education and education in human rights as part of the effort to reform and develop education. They assign special status in the national educational system to women, scheduled castes, scheduled tribes, minorities, and the handicapped, and emphasize values education. They also define the basic components of the core curriculum, which reflects some important human rights concerns. The National Curriculum Framework is provided for by the 1986 National Education Policy. It covers core elements that cut across narrow subject boundaries and is designed to promote values such as India's common cultural heritage, egalitarianism, democracy, secularism, equality of the sexes, observance of small-family norms, and inculcation of scientific temper, among other things.

Human rights education is significant as an instrument of raising awareness of human rights. Of the world's school children, about 77% are in primary school, and of these, 68% are girls. As per the Annual Report of UNICEF, 130 million primary-school-age children in the developing world are denied the right to basic and quality education; 70 million are girls (40 million of whom are Indian girls). It is lamentable that in the early 1990s, more than one quarter of the 95 million school children in developing countries did not reach the fifth grade. Most countries failed to achieve universal access to education by year 2000. Human rights education is not a mere vision. It will become a way of life. It is necessary if nonformal education is to prepare millions of children to be good world citizens. A framework to support nonformal human rights education has to be developed.

Schooling provides not only basic education but also, under the best circumstances, aids a child to explore the world and express ideas. The school can help establish an intellectual basis for teaching the historical development of human rights and their contemporary significance. This knowledge should ultimately extend beyond the pupils immediate environment and culture. Human rights should be presented in the context of a society's moral and social traditions. The school is not just for transmitting a national ideology and a common historical memory through the curriculum. On a deeper level, like the political nation, the school forms a constructed place in which students, like citizens, are treated equally, irrespective of their background.

The concept of the school is like the "concept of citizenship, impersonal and formal. By understanding the idea of school as a community, citizens will learn to understand and feel included in the political nation" The school is a model of good society as John Dewey suggested. Schools are places where it is theoretically possible to operate a community based on social justice and human rights. The climate of a school should encourage open expression of views and dialogue between students and teachers. The school can work toward building a closer relationship between itself and the community.

Human rights should permeate the whole school-from its ethos and organization to the content of its curriculum. The first National Curriculum Framework formulated by the National Council of Educational Research and Training (NCERT) in 1975 states: "The awakening of social consciousness, the development of democratic values and of a feeling for social injustice and national integration are extremely important" All subjects should be taught in such a manner so as to foster the spirit of scientific humanism.? The National Curriculum Framework for primary and secondary education identifies and addresses some of these concerns such as promoting values of egalitarianism, democracy, secularism, equality, removal of social barriers, and creating a sense of common citizenship.

It proposes that the school curriculum reflects some world issues and helps make children become aware of and appreciate different world cultures. Highlighting the need to strengthen national identity, the National Curriculum Framework for School Education reaffirms the 10 core components identified in the National Policy on Education:

— the history of India's freedom movement;

— Constitutional obligations;

— the content essential to nurture national identity;

— India's common cultural heritage;

— egalitarianism;

— democracy and secularism;

— equality of the sexes;

— protection of the environment;

— removal of social barriers;

— observance of small-family norms; and

— inculcation of scientific temper.

It further emphasizes the need to include the fundamental duties as laid down in Article 51 A of Part IV A of the Constitution as common core components of the curriculum: "These core components need to be integrated in school curriculum in a suitable manner. It is envisaged that they would help in instilling a nationally shared perception and values and creating an ethos and value system in which a common Indian identity could be strengthened.

Curriculum Development

Curriculum development includes curriculum planning, formulation of curriculum policy, implementation, and evaluation. The process of curriculum renewal has to be continuous to accommodate new developments and changes in various subjects. The curriculum development exercises should be undertaken as a systematically planned improvement strategy based on accepted foundational principles. Human rights education should not only be incorporated into the formal curriculum as a separate subject but also integrated into the entire curriculum, including the hidden curriculum (i.e., the culture of schooling and teacher training institutions and programs).

Human rights teaching materials should be produced in different forms. There should be no separate human rights curriculum. Rather, human rights dimensions can be integrated into the existing curriculum. The heart of human rights education is curriculum development for all stages of school education. The curriculum should incorporate valuable ideas from the Vienna Declaration-human rights, humanitarian law, democracy, rule of law, peace, development, and social justice. We can add many more to provide local color and to relate human rights with the needs of learners at different stages. Maybe some of these topics are already in the curriculum, but now the challenge is to make the topics the main agenda of learning.

Human rights education aims to do the following:

— Enhance the knowledge and understanding of human rights.

— Foster attitudes of tolerance, respect, solidarity, and responsibility.

— Develop awareness of how human rights can be translated into social and political reality.

— Develop skills for protecting human rights.

The design of the curriculum needs to be built on the philosophical, psychological, and sociological bases of curriculum planning and development. The school curriculum should work toward the holistic development of the individual. Human rights education can be incorporated into the school curriculum in several ways:

— The formal curriculum: Schools may choose to examine their present curriculums and identify areas where themes and elements of human rights education already exist. Human rights education is considered the most important part of the core curriculum of good general education.

— The informal curriculum: Human rights education can also be promoted through the extracurricular and co-curricular activities of the school.

— The hidden curriculum: Human rights education should also address the farreaching hidden curriculum of the school to create a school atmosphere that truly reflects respect for human rights. Values, attitudes, knowledge, and patterns of behavior should be integrated into the students personal experiences in order to help them view reality critically.

Context and Approaches

The contexts of and approaches to incorporating human rights education in the curriculum are the following:

— *Direct context*: This involves including specific topics or subjects that focus on human rights education into mathematics, science, or history subjects, for example. India has introduced human rights education at the higher education levels. Recently, the Indira Gandhi National Open University (IGNOU) started a certificate course in human rights education.

— *Indirect context*: This involves the use of all school subjects as vehicles for human rights education. Some examples are

(i) creating "learning units in human rights" in order to integrate the content of different subjects toward solving a particular problem and

(ii) including human rights elements in every subject.

— *Implicit context*: This involves the creation of a sociocultural ethos in schools that will develop students understanding of human rights.

The question is how to introduce the new curriculums at various levels. It is obvious that one more subject cannot be added to an already overloaded curriculum, as it would constitute a violation of human rights of sorts. Human rights education should be integrated into existing curriculums. The question, however, is what and how much is to be integrated. The answer requires a selection of issues. Teaching the basic rights may be done under the umbrella of ethics. At the secondary level, basic and other rights may be introduced into existing foundation courses.

The first question in curriculum building is in what way human rights issues can be structured and elaborated upon at different levels. The curriculum, among other things, stresses the following core values:

— *Issues of human rights and democracy*:

(i) dignity;

(ii) equality;

(iii) justice;

(iv) protection of rights;

(v) freedom of participation;

(vi) freedom of speech and expression; and

(vii) freedom of religious belief.

— *Values and attitudes*:

(i) human rights and democracy;

(ii) cooperation and solidarity;

(iii) preservation of culture;

(iv) self and others;

(v) internationalism;

(vi) protection of the environment; and

(vii) spirituality.

These values are deemed universally acceptable and desirable in such documents as the Declaration, the Convention on the Rights of the Child, the Convention on the Elimination of Discrimination against Women, etc. Human rights education is interdisciplinary. The central area may be outlined as follows:

— education for tolerance;

— democracy and national understanding;

— protection of human rights;

- violation of human rights and democratic freedom;
- economic rights;
- civil rights;
- critical thinking;
- scientific temper;
- intellectual honesty;
- justice and empathy;
- legal awareness;
- equality of educational opportunity;
- gender equality;
- political economy and humanism;
- minority rights;
- local government and civic rights;
- constitutionalism and legitimacy;
- history and philosophy of human rights;
- world citizenship;
- role of the UN;
- human rights and national and world histories;
- international understanding; and
- environmental protection.

Human rights education should focus on attitudes of tolerance, respect, and solidarity, and develop individual awareness of how human rights can be translated into social and political reality.

The basic approach to human rights education in schools is to integrate it into various subjects and not treat it as a separate area of study. It also requires a multidisciplinary approach. The issue of human rights is inextricably linked with other major curricular issues. The National Curriculum

Framework for School Education recommends the integration of various curricular concerns:

The curriculum development process is often influenced by a 'panic approach in which the local, national or international developments with some socio-economic and political bearing influence the decisions concerning the curriculum without prior, careful and structured planning. This 'panic approach' of including new and temporal curricular concerns may often lead to an overloading of the curriculum. At a time when concerns such as 'literacy' 'family system', 'neighborhood education', 'environmental education', 'consumer education', 'tourism education', 'AIDS education', 'human rights education', 'legal literacy', 'peace education', 'population education', 'migration education', 'global education',and 'safety education' are making a case for separate place in the school curriculum, the best approach would be to integrate these ideas and concepts, after a careful analysis in the existing areas of learning.

Appropriate strategies for this integration may be suitably worked out in the detailed subject curricula. It is vital to examine the learning opportunities available when designing new curriculum or introducing specific changes so as to avoid a disparity between expectation and reality. This should constitute a realistic approach -meaningful, responsive, and result oriented. Human rights is itself an educational conception involving human interaction inside and outside school.

Human rights education is not treated as a separate area of the curriculum but is integrated into various subjects at different stages:

— the Indian political system and Constitution;

— problems and challenges of contemporary life-political, economic, social, cultural, educational-that have direct or indirect bearing on human rights;

— diversity and variety of Indian culture, its composite and non-monolithic character;

- — the Indian social system and dynamics of social change;
- — major events in Indian and world history relating to the struggle for political and civil rights as well as economic and social rights, and the role of the people and outstanding leaders in these struggles;
- — the world human rights situation with regard to gross violations in the form of colonialism, racism, and apartheid; and
- — literary works that reflect human rights concerns and the quest for freedom and rights.

Major historical documents such as the American Declaration of Independence, the French Declaration of the Rights of Man and the Citizen, the UN Charter, and the Universal Declaration of Human Rights should be discussed. It is imperative to discuss the human rights curriculum as a cross-curricular approach at the elementary and secondary levels. The major subject areas relevant to human rights at the lower-primary stage are social studies, environmental studies, and languages.

- — Human rights issues are integrated into environmental studies, starting with the child's immediate environment and gradually taking the child to the study of the district, state, country, and the world.
- — Narratives and biographies of men and women from the history of India and of the world, India's freedom struggle, and certain aspects of the Indian Constitution should be included in this course.
- — The language curriculum should focus on the development of compassion, tolerance, and sympathy, through stories and poems.
- — Environmental studies dealing with family, neighborhood, relations, food, clothing, shelter, religious festivals, and national heroes expand the knowledge of and respect for diversity and human equality.

— Children also develop an understanding of independent India as it evolved during the freedom struggle. Learning about the nation's goals and the main features of the Constitution-fundamental rights, directive principles of State policy, and fundamental duties, as well as secularism and democracy-may help promote human rights.

In the upper-primary stage, the major subject areas relevant to human rights education are social studies, science, and languages.

— History courses deal mainly with Indian history and, in general, with the history of world civilization, stressing an understanding and appreciation of India's cultural heritage and composite nature, its richness and variety. They focus on understanding diversity and consideration for other's rights.

— The human rights dimension lies in providing a critical understanding of Indian society through the ages, with focus on the position of women and the inequalities created by the caste system.

— Children should be made aware of legislative reforms and the role of international organizations in uplifting women and children.

— The course in geography helps children develop an appreciation for different ways of living, interdependence, and sharing of common values by diverse cultures.

Civics helps promote values of democracy, secularism, socialism, and national integration. It also includes the study of issues relating the environment, arms race, and human rights. Children develop a perspective of these problems in an international context. It is possible to introduce the student to a more comprehensive view of the concept of human rights and the interconnection between the ideals of secularism and democracy.

— The thematic and ideational content in language help to promote awareness of human rights, international understanding, and related issues of global significance. The subject of language similarly lays the foundation for an appreciation of the underlying humanistic values conveyed through folk tales, legends, poems, essays, and dramas.

— Science is an undiversified subject. Stress is on inculcating a national outlook and thereby helping to combat obscurantism and prejudice based on narrow consideration of caste, sex, or religion. The course guidelines also emphasize promoting understanding of the processes and problem areas related to agriculture, health and nutrition, environmental protection, energy, material resources, and, more important, developing a scientific attitude.

Secondary schools offer a much wider and varied range of opportunities to teach human rights and to practice and observe rights and duties.

— A literature course may offer the opportunity to study the rights of children and young people. Literature and language classes can be used to promote cultural exchanges with schools in other countries as well as to promote social relations, peace, freedom, and justice.

— At this stage, "the global perspective" and "major concerns" are integrated into the social sciences.

Human rights can be taught in the context and understanding of the following:

— "small"society-family life, school, and community;

— the "big"society-community, country, and State;

— forms of government-democratic, dictatorship, parliamentary;

— the United Nations;

— the world today-East-West problems, armaments, events, and personalities in international affairs;

— the world around us-studies of individual countries;

— the family and society-economic, political, and cultural interdependence; and

— religion and philosophy of life-What do we believe in? Analysis of different religions, traditional beliefs, and practices.

History allows the study of human rights as it covers topics such as the growth of democracy, development of trade unions, social reforms, and independence movements. The Industrial Revolution, and its impact on countries outside Europe, might be linked with the study of the International Labour Organization and its efforts to ensure just and equitable conditions for all workers, and to abolish child labor and other abuses of human dignity. It also introduces the students to some of the significant declarations on human rights, from the American Declaration of Independence to the Universal Declaration of Human Rights.

— Geography stresses environmental and pollution issues and the study of international ecological problems.

— Civics focuses on Indian democracy, including topics such as the individual and society, democratic citizenship, the Constitution, the judiciary, democracy, foreign policy, the UN, world problems (human rights, disarmament, new international order, etc.).

— Economics focuses mainly on the study of the Indian economy-economic development and social justice-by covering content areas such as the rights of consumers, and consumer protection.

— Science stresses the development of scientific temper; cultivation of social, ethi-cal, and social values; and the possible misuse of science. Biology can explore the scientific bases for human rights and social prejudice. Science can also include teaching of health, diseases, and the contribution of the World Health Organization.

— Mathematics can teach the skills related to elementary statistics and graphing, which may be used to interpret data on food and population, agriculture and industrial outputs, expenditure on armaments and on education, and other topics that have a bearing on basic human rights. Natural science and mathematics also reflect the modern scientific and technological work that may either benefit humankind or work to its detriment.

Teaching Human Rights through Co-curricular Activities

Human rights education goes beyond subject teaching to organization of other activities and should be considered as an integral part of the whole education process. Activities that promote cooperation and group living can include human rights content. Teachers can involve elementary-school children in creative tasks such as paper cutting, drawing, collage, and work related to science, environmental studies, and social studies. Exhibitions, displays, and debates on human rights issues should be considered as core elements of human rights education. The activities themselves lead to an understanding of human rights as the children learn to cooperate and respect each other.

Theater and literacy activities should be part of human rights education. Role play is an important strategy for inculcating values in children. Even the study of major literary and artistic works may promote human rights education, international understanding, and peace. International-relations clubs, art, music or drama circles, and UNESCO and United Nations clubs promote international understanding. Activities such as putting up wall newspapers and posters on current events, holding debates, writing essays and poems, celebrating special days such as Human Rights Day and World Health Day, and activities relating to population, apartheid, literacy, etc. inculcate human rights values and generate awareness of human rights.

Human rights education projects can be taken up in any discipline-history, geography, civics, literature, and science, etc. Human rights teaching should permeate not only all school subjects but also every aspect of school life. There is no denying the fact that human rights can be taught more effectively through various cocurricular activities. The methodological issues are relatively more important than the content as far as human rights education is concerned. Teaching methods are crucial in sensitizing and changing attitudes and creating a human rights culture. As the current teaching methodology may reduce human rights education to a mere academic exercise, it is important to bring field experiences into the classroom and take students to the communities.

Teacher attitudes and assessment methods are important in conveying key messages to students. It is also important that the practices adopted in schools and the classroom reflects a climate and culture of human rights. The flesh and blood of schooling-the relationship among students, teachers, and school administrators, and teaching strategies-need to be rebuilt on the basic philosophy of human rights.

Importance of Teachers and Teacher Education

Teachers are clearly important in human rights education. Can they teach with uniform proficiency? What about teachers who are not even aware of their rights and duties in the classroom? Simply, they are to be trained in content as well as pedagogy, material preparation, and curriculum development as they have to be role models. It is the most effective way to improve the quality and effectiveness of human rights education programs. They should be provided with the knowledge, skills, and understanding to inculcate human rights as part of their teacher education courses at both the pre- and in-service levels. Empowerment of teachers and parents is also a key issue that should be tackled and worked out at all levels of government. Education should be considered a duty not a right. Otherwise, the Declaration will become a mere subject of academic study.

PLANNING FOR THE FUTURE

In planning for the future, it is assumed, obviously, that the goal of an education policy would be to universalise primary education (age group 5-9) and upper primary education (age group 10-14 years). Apart from this, that a 75 % enrolment rate is to be achieved in higher secondary (age group 15-19) and 20 % enrolment in colleges and professional education (age group 20-24).

The age-wise population projections for 2015 of the US Census Bureau (Table 1) have been utilised to arrive at the school going population. In making these projections, all prices and costs are based on 1998-99 levels.

Table 1
India's popultion profile (in Million)

Age Group	Year 2000	Year 2015
0-4	117	115
5-9	113	113
10-14	111	113
15-19	103	113
20-24	94	110
25-29	84	109
30-34	76	100
35-39	67	90
40-44	58	81
45-49	49	72
50-54	40	62
55-59	32	51
60-64	24	40
65-69	18	30
70-74	14	20
75-79	8	12
80+	6	10
Total	1014	1241

Source: US Census Bureau

Enrolment of Students in 2015

The estimated enrolment of students by the year 2015 will be 1130 lakhs in primary school, 1130 lakhs in upper primary, 1130 lakhs in secondary and 220 lakhs in colleges/university. The number of students in each age group in the respective level of education is presented in Table 2.

Table 2

Estimated demand for education by year 2015 (in Million)

Particulars	
School-going population (5-19 years)	339
Primary (5-9 years)	113
Upper Primary (10-14 years)	113
Potential Secondary (15-19 years)	113
Estimated Secondary (75% of potential secondary)	85
Potential college-going population (20-24 years)	110
Estimated college-going population (20% of potential college-going)	22

Number of Education Institutions

To achieve the above enrolments, the number of schools and institutions needs to be increased manifold from the current levels. Based on 150 students in a primary school, the additional number of primary schools would be 7,32,000 schools, double the number today. Assuming 675 students in each secondary school, additional 23,600 schools would be required. At the tertiary level, additional 27,000 institutions, almost three times the existing number, would be required with 580 students in each institution. The details of the total educational institutions required are presented in Table 3.

Table 3
Estimated demand for schools/institutions by the year 2015
(numbers)

	Total required	Existing (1996)	Additional required
Primary	1506,667	775,000	731,667
Secondary	125,556	102,000	23,556
Tertiary	37,931	10,460	27,471

Source: Reliance Research

Recurring Expenditure

Recurring expenditure is in the form of establishment expenses, teacher salaries, textbooks and training material. The annual recurring expenditure that would be required to meet the above objectives would be around 11% of the current GNP and 3.15 % of the projected GNP. This translates to Rs.1,80,000 crores each year. The compulsory and free education level (age group 5-14) would account for about 37 % (Rs. 65,850 crores) of the total expenditure. The public spending would be 1.98 % of the projected GNP. The details of the recurring expenditure are presented in Table 4.

Table 4.
Estimated recurring expenditure in 2015 at 1998-99 prices
(Rs. crores)

A.	School-going population (5-19)	
i.	Primary (5-9)	65,850
ii.	Secondary (15-19)	73,022
B.	College-going population (20-24)	41207
	Total Expenditure (A (i+ii) + B)	180,079
	GNP for 1998-99	16,12,383
	Recurring expenditure as a % of GNP	11.16%

Source : Reliance Research

Capital Expenditure

Capital expenditure pertains to cost of buildings, furniture and fixtures, toilets,. communication equipment, computers etc. Capital costs to fund the incremental number of institutions required have been assumed taking an average cost of Rs. 10 lakhs for a primary institution, Rs. 20 lakhs for a secondary institution and Rs. 40 lakhs for a tertiary institution. On this basis, the total capital expenditure required will be Rs.88,900 crores.

It is reasonable to assume that this required capital investment would be met over the next 15 years. Thus the annual capital expenditure will be Rs. 5,900 crores. The computation of capital costs is presented in Table 5.

Table 5

Estimated captial costs at 1998-99 Prices

	Additional required (numbers)	Capital Cost (Rs. per unit)	Total (Rs. crores)	Required capital investment (Rs. crores)
Primary	7,31,667	10,00,000	73,167	4,878
Secondary	23,556	2,00,000	4,711	314
Tertiary	27,471	40,00,000	10,988	732
Total			88,866	5,924

Source: Reliance Research

Public and Private Spend on Education

The total expenditure has been separated as those that would be spent by the government and that would be spent by the private sources. The percentages of public spending would be 90 % in the primary sector, 50 % in the secondary sector and 40 % in the tertiary sector. This would translate to a total public spending of Rs. 1,17,000 crores and a private spending of Rs. 68,900 crores. In effect this means that the government would spend 63 % of the total expenditure. The private sector would spend the rest. The government spend would be 1.98 % of the projected GNP. The details of the public and private investments in education are presented in Table 6.

Table 6
Estimated breakup of private and public sectors investments (2015)

	Share of public investment	Share of private investment	Public investment	Private investment
	Percent	Percent	Rs. crores	Rs. crores
Recurring				
Primary	90	10	59,265	6,585
Secondary	50	50	36,511	36,511
Tertiary	40	60	16,483	24,724
Non-recurring				
Primary	90	10	4,390	488
Secondary	50	50	157	157
Tertiary	40	60	293	439
Total				
Primary			63,655	7,073
Secondary			36,668	36,668
Tertiary			16,776	25,163
Grand total			117,099	68,904

Source: Reliance Research

Manpower Requirements for Tertiary Education Planning

Three scenarios have been presented, one where India would achieve a GNP growth of 6 percent (pessimistic), 8 percent (most likely) and 10 percent (optimistic). The requirements of professionals in various sectors are based on the growth in GNP.

In the case of engineers, the growth rate in manufacturing sector and its contribution to the economy is taken into consideration. The assumptions are that agriculture will constitute 20 percent of GDP, manufacturing and services will constitute 40 percent each. Estimates of GNP growth under the three scenarios are given in Table 7.

Table 7
GNP Forecast of India (Real terms at 1998-99 Prices)
(Rs. billion)

GNP growth	6%(Pessimistic)	8% (Most likely)	10% (Optimistic)
1998-99	15974.16	15974.16	15974.16
1999-00	16932.61	17252.09	17571.58
2000-01	17948.57	18632.26	19328.73
2001-02	19025.48	20122.84	21261.61
2002-03	20167.01	21732.67	23387.77
2003-04	21377.03	23471.28	25726.54
2004-05	22659.65	25348.98	28299.20
2005-06	24019.23	27376.90	31129.12
2006-07	25460.38	29567.06	34242.03
2007-08	26988.01	31932.42	37666.23
2008-09	28607.29	34487.01	41432.86
2009-10	30323.72	37245.97	45576.14
2010-11	32143.15	40225.65	50133.76
2011-12	34071.74	43443.70	55147.13
2012-13	36116.04	46919.20	60661.85
2013-14	38283.00	50672.74	66728.03
2014-15	40579.98	54726.56	73400.83
2015-16	43014.78	59104.68	80740.92

Source: Base figure: Economic Survey 2000;
Estimates: BIU, Chennai

In the case of doctors, including dentists and veterinary doctors and nurses, who are involved in providing healthcare services, an idealistic target number of doctors and nurses per 1000 population based on international human development statistics were relied upon.

The estimates indicate that the total population that should have achieved tertiary education will between 5.6 % and 9.8 %. The total number of teachers in all the sectors would need to increase from the existing 49.25 lakhs to a range of 93.47 lakhs to 119.15 lakhs. The details are presented in Table 8.

OPTIONS IN FINANCING AND MANAGEMENT

Present systems for financing and managing education are often inappropriate for meeting the challenges of ensuring equity in education amongst disadvantaged groups, ensuring quality of education and for speeding up reforms in the education system. Public financing is growing more difficult as enrolments expand. Public intervention in education can be justified on several counts: it can reduce inequality, open opportunities for the poor and the disadvantaged, compensate for market failures in lending for education, and make information about the benefits and availability of education generally available. But public spending on education is often inefficient and inequitable. It is inefficient when it is misallocated among uses; it is inequitable when qualified potential students are unable to enrol in institutions because educational opportunities are lacking or because of the inability to pay.

The inefficiencies and inequities, along with expanding enrolments in public schools at all levels, have contributed to increasing the share of GNP devoted to public spending on education. The result is increasing pressure on public funds.

To merely increase efficiency in public spending on education may not be enough. The government will necessarily have to increase the quantum of public spending.

This can be done in several ways. Government can reallocate public spending to education from other publicly funded activities such as defence and inefficient public sector enterprises. Government can increase revenues and spend more on education. Government can also supplement public funds for education with private funds.

Private financing can be encouraged either to fund private institutions or to supplement the income of publicly funded institutions. Private schools and universities tend to draw their students from more advantaged socio-economic backgrounds, and thereby promote diversity and provide useful competition for public institutions, especially at higher levels of education.

Policy Options in Financing Education

Adverse macroeconomic conditions and keen inter-sectoral competition for public funds have reduced the Indian government's ability to continue expanding education. The lack of a credit market for education makes this problem worse. There are basically three policy options that could overcome some of the problems in financing education. These options are:

Recovering the public cost of higher education and reallocating government spending on education towards the level with the highest social returns

Developing a credit market for education, together with selective scholarships, especially in higher education

Decentralising the management of public education and encouraging the expansion of private and community-supported schools.

Public Investment in Education

The high rates of return estimated for basic education in most developing countries strongly suggest that investments to improve enrolments and retention in basic education should generally have the highest priority in India, which has not yet

Table 8

Projection of manpower for tertiary education

		Required resource if GDP growth is			Required rate of compounded annual growth to reach the desired level		
	Existing Resource	6%	8%	10%	6%	8%	10%
	1998	Pessimistic	Most Likeiy	Optimistic	Pessimistic	Most Likely	Optimistic
				Percent			Nos.
	(1)	(2)	(3)	(4)	(2)/(1) ^ (1/16)-1	(3)/(1) ^ (1/16)-1	(4)/(1) ^ (1/16)-1
Prof-essionals	2,854,545	15,270,074	20,981,922	28,662,698	11.05	13.28	15.51
Engineers	2,053,900	8,849,098	12,159,147	16,610,202	9.56	11.76	13.96
Scientists	126,945	2,756,701	3,787,859	5,174,467	21.21	23.64	26.08
Doctors	359,700	1,263,543	1,736,178	2,371,734	8.17	10.34	12.51
Dentists	20,700	63,177	86,809	118,587	7.22	9.37	11.53
Veterinary doctors	42,700	126,354	173,618	237,173	7.02	9.16	11.31
Nurses	250,600	2,211,200	3,038,311	4,150,534	14.58	16.88	19.18
Grad-uates	15,180,200	65,134,465	89,498,341	122,260,675	9.53	11.73	13.93

Arts	7,663,100	32,880,457	45,179,559	61,718,276	9.53	11.73	13.93
Science	3,479,300	14,928,812	20,513,009	28,022,132	9.53	11.73	13.93
Comm-erce	4,037,800	17,325,196	23,805,773	32,520,267	9.53	11.73	13.93
Post-graduates	4,765,300	20,446,718	28,094,916	38,379,520	9.53	11.73	13.93
Arts	3,341,300	14,336,688	19,699,398	26,910,686	9.53	11.73	13.93
Science	695,500	2,984,218	4,100,479	5,601,527	9.53	11.73	13.93
Commerce	728,500	3,125,812	4,295,038	5,867,308	9.53	11.73	13.93
Total population in the tertiary level	22,800,045	100,851,257	138,575,179	189,302,894	9.74	11.94	14.14
% of population required to achieve tertiary education as % of total population	2.38%	5.68%	7.80%	10.65%	5.59	7.71	9.83

Teachers	4,925,154	9,347,440	10,465,173	11,914,832	4.09	4.82	5.68
Primary	3,083,345	5,685,944	6,498,221	7,581,258	3.90	4.77	5.78
Secondary	1,521,186	2,457,986	2,621,852	2,809,127	3.04	3.46	3.91
Tertiary	320,623	1,203,511	1,345,100	1,524,447	8.62	9.38	10.24

Source: Base figures: Institute of Applied Manpower Research; estimates: BIU, Chennai

achieved universal basic education. A policy package in respect of the role of the public sector in education would consist of:

— Free basic education, including cost-sharing with local communities and targeted stipends for children from poor households

— Selective charging of fees for upper-secondary education, combined with targeted scholarships.

— Fees for all public higher education, combined with loans, taxes, and other schemes to allow needy students to defer payment until they become income-earners, and a targeted scholarship scheme to overcome the reluctance of the poor to accumulate debt against uncertain future earnings.

— Assurance of quality primary education for all children by making that level the top priority for public spending on education.

— Improved access to quality general secondary education as the second priority, once all children are receiving good primary education.

— Efficient Public Spending at the School and Institution Level

Public finance is the main instrument for implementing public priorities, and there is a strong rationale for public intervention in the financing of education. The high private rates of return to investments at all levels of education justify large investments by individuals. They also justify self-financing by families or students, through immediate or deferred cost sharing. Despite these high private returns and the justification for private finance, there is also a strong case for public intervention, especially for basic education, for reasons of income distribution, capital market imperfections, information asymmetries, and externalities.

In fact most governments are heavily involved in all levels of education - an activity that takes up a significant portion of public expenditure. Education expenditure by source of funds in some important countries is given in Table 9.

Table 9.
Education expendtiure by source of funds , all levels of education combined (1991)

Group and country	Public sources	Private sources
OECD		
Australia	85.0	15.0
Canada	90.1	9.9
Denmark	99.4	0.6
Finland	92.3	7.7
France	89.7	10.3
Germany	72.9	27.1
Ireland	93.4	6.6
Japan	73.9	26.1
Netherlands	98.0	2.0
Spain	80.1	19.9
United States	78.6	21.4
Low-and middle-income countries		
Haiti	20.0	80.0
Hungary	93.1	6.9
India	89.0	11.0
Indonesia	62.8	37.2
Kenya	62.2	37.8
Uganda	43.0	57.0
Venezuela	73.0	27.0

Source: Priorities and strategies for education - A World Bank review 1995

Private Financing as an Incentive Mechanism

The general expectation is that the more a school depends on private financing, through fees collected from students or contributions from the local community, or both, the more the school is likely to use resources efficiently. When people share directly in the cost of a service, they are likely to monitor costs more closely and guard against waste. Even when public institutions charge no fees, allowing fee-charging private institutions to emerge and survive can generate the incentive for greater efficiency. Such institutions promote competition in the system and generate information for judging the performance of public institutions.

Financing Upper-Secondary Education and Higher Education

Since secondary school graduates will have higher earnings than those who leave school earlier, selectively charging fees for public secondary school can help to increase enrolments. Cost sharing with communities can be encouraged at the secondary level. There is considerable evidence that household demand for education is relatively price-inelastic, that is, unresponsive to increases in private costs, except among the poor. The relative inelasticity of demand could be a useful criterion for making decisions about charging fees. However, poorer families have difficulty in meeting the direct and indirect costs of children's school attendance. To offset this hardship, secondary school fees can be combined with scholarships and stipends to ensure equity in enrolment.

In general, fees are justified at public institutions for higher education. An optimal policy would be full cost recovery by public higher education institutions, with students paying fees out of parental income and out of their own future incomes, through a loan scheme or a graduate tax. Such a policy is very distant in India since existing fee levels are so low and experience with loan schemes has been relatively disappointing.

An extremely radical cost-saving intervention is distance education. Distance education is dramatically cheaper than conventional higher education. But lower unit costs do not necessarily imply greater efficiency in open universities, because completion rates often are also lower. One reason is that open universities tend to attract weaker students because entry is usually non-competitive. Another reason is that, with only a tenuous link to an institution, teachers and fellow students, a student's motivation and discipline to complete a course is poorly reinforced. Even though open universities produce graduates efficiently, the output is wasted unless graduates are productive in the labour market.

Credit Market for Education

Without well-functioning commercial credit markets, people must often borrow funds from relatives, friends and moneylenders. These sources of credit are inefficient since the ability to borrow depends on whom the borrower knows and whether willing lenders can be found.

Extensive financial regulation generally limits total supply of loans in the economy, and private banks may be unwilling to lend to students. Education is a particularly long-term investment, and risks are high because few students have acceptable collateral. Graduates may be unable to repay loans if they are ill or unemployed. India also lacks the legal and administrative framework to enforce financial contracts effectively.

The government can play an important role in alleviating students' difficulties in obtaining educational credit. The government is big enough to absorb risks that private lenders cannot or will not bear, by insuring commercially loaned funds from banks. If loans are under government authority, employers may also be willing to make deduction from former students' salaries for loan repayment. Some types of loans, especially for medical studies, could be repaid through national service in deprived areas of the country. The extensive network of more than 66,000 branches of commercial banks could be used effectively for government-guaranteed student loan administration.

Student Loan Schemes

Introducing loans for higher education adds benefits on almost all counts. Loans mobilise more resources for higher education by tapping graduates' future earnings, even when default rates and administrative costs of loan schemes are high. They improve resource allocation because students will tend to enrol in the courses with the highest returns. When augmented by selective scholarships, loans improve student selection and equity by allowing talented students from poor families to compete for places in higher education.

Student loan schemes are an essential complement to cost recovery and the charging of fees. Many students are unable to afford the cost of higher education out of their families' current income, and loan schemes permit them to pay out of their future earnings. About fifty countries, industrial and developing, have such schemes. In most countries, loans are repaid according to a fixed schedule; in a few, including Australia and Sweden, they are repaid as a proportion of a graduate's income each year.

In the United States, student loan programmes guaranteed by the government enable borrowing from abroad also. Loan schemes can be made financially sustainable, as the experiences of Canada and Colombia demonstrate. They require the public sector to bear some of the risk, since banks and financial institutions are generally unwilling to accept students' likely future earnings as collateral.

Sustainable loan schemes require an effective collection agency with incentives to minimise evasion and default. Income-contingent and graduated annual payment schemes are needed to encourage repayment commensurate with the students' future earnings, which will rise over time.

Role of Non-Governmental Organisations (NGOs)

The contribution that NGOs can make to efforts to expand access and improve the quality of education is immense. The Bangladesh Rural Advancement Committee (BRAC) is a shining instance of an NGO playing a national role in the country's health and population programmes. In 1992, BRAC had more than 8,000 schools operating, and plans are being made to expand to 50,000 schools. The education programme is free to students, except for community contributions for school construction.

Internationally, BRAC is a model for the potential of the NGO sector in education expansion. It also illustrates how a combination of targeting, school design, flexibility and follow-through can dramatically increase girls' primary school participation rates. NGOs have greater flexibility than government bureaucracies and may be able to reach target groups more effectively. Furthermore, as BRAC's expansion programme illustrates, NGOs need not necessarily be limited to small pilot projects, but can also carry out large-scale delivery programmes.

NGOs have long been pioneers in the area of early child development. Save the Children, for instance, is an international NGO that has worked with at-risk children and families since 1932 and is now active in forty countries world-wide. The Aga Khan Foundation is working in parts of Pakistan and with Muslim communities on the coast of Kenya. The Soros Foundation focuses a large share of its resources on pre-school education in Eastern Europe and Central Asia.

Revenue Diversification

Encouraging public educational institutions to diversify their sources of revenue and allowing them to keep such revenues can encourage autonomy. The scope for this is greatest in higher education. The practice of attracting resources from alumni and private industry is standard among private schools and universities, and is beginning to spread to public ones. In Chile, Indonesia, Thailand and Venezuela, private industry provides scholarships or subsidised loans for talented university students. Structured tax regimes can encourage such donations.

Public schools and universities can also use their facilities to provide income. Universities in Uganda and Senegal generate 4 to 5 percent of annual expenditure by renting out facilities. China and Vietnam encourage schools to run short-term courses, and provide services to industry.

Quality of Education and Education Expenditure

Schooling within formal education systems plays an important role in the expansion of human capital. However, there is a big difference between children sitting in a classroom and an increase in human capital. The quality of education is a deep concern in India. If the quality deficiencies were due merely to the lack of inputs the policy prescription would be obvious: increase resources. However, empirical evidence shows that resources are only tenuously related to measured achievement.

Budgets do not account for performance, how well a budget is spent plays an important role. There is clear evidence that the enormous inefficiencies in education spending arise due to relatively high spending on teacher inputs. In a study made in Northeast Brazil, it was found that cost effectiveness of teacher salaries (normalised to one) is by far the lowest. Material inputs that provide amenities to the school and teachers, such as teacher tables, toilets, bookcases, have a cost effectiveness on average 7.7 times larger than teacher salaries.

Instructional materials have cost effectiveness ratios between 17 and 34 times as large as the impact of additional spending on teacher salary increases. A World Bank study in India covering eight states has come to similar conclusions. The cost effectiveness of spending on improving physical facilities is higher than that of teacher salaries (1.2 times higher), however that for increasing just classroom size is between 1.7 and 4 times higher. The cost effectiveness of spending on instructional inputs is between 4 and 14 times higher than that of increasing teacher salaries.

UNIVERSAL BASIC EDUCATION

Every time the country talks of improving the quality of education or universalising elementary education, it is suggested that a shortage of resources is a strong obstacle to progress. The truth is different. It is not a matter of resources but of priorities.

Poorer countries than India have achieved much more in education. War-torn Vietnam with a per capita income of under $300 has achieved a literacy rate of 94 per cent. Kenya, with a per capita income of $340 has achieved a literacy rate of 75 percent. India with a per capita income of $390 has a literacy rate of 62 per cent.

India also needs to improve the efficiency of public spending on education. It spends around 3.5 per cent of its gross national product (GNP) on education - a much higher share than China and Sri Lanka - but its educational achievements are lower. Sri Lanka, which spends only 3.1 percent of its GNP on education, has ensured that 90 percent of adults are literate and that 98 percent of children complete primary school.

China spends only 2.3 percent of its GNP on education, and 82 per cent of its adults are literate, while 94 percent of those who enter school complete primary schooling. Vietnam spends only 2.6 percent of its GNP on education, yet, as already mentioned, the literacy level is 94 percent.

University Partnership

The universities must be strongly encouraged to form partnerships with industry. Such a linkage would entail several benefits for the university. It would give the university opportunities to attract additional funds for teaching and research thereby facilitating financial autonomy, access to latest technology, improved employment prospects for students, continuous upgradation and adaptation of curriculum and improved motivation in students.

The industry would also stand to benefit through reduction in recruiting costs, access to pre-screened, high achieving students, cost effective productivity, better communications with the higher learning centres and collaborative research opportunities.

Students stand to gain in the form of real life practical experience, contact with practising professionals, and application of theoretical knowledge and enhancement of oral and written skills.

Network and Infrastructure Planning

Planning networks and establishing networks among neighbourhood villages offer a potent possibility in this era of modern communications facilities and the Internet. It is physically and economically viable to link villages using wide area networks and provide community Internet centres. All teaching can originate from the 'hub' villages for dissemination simultaneously to a number of villages. The advantages of such a network are basically two. One, the pupil-teacher ratio can be raised to a new high, without unduly affecting the quality of education. Two, timing can be kept flexible so as to involve the entire household in the education process.

7

SOCIAL DEVELOPMENT THROUGH HIGHER EDUCATION

Ancient records of the Indian tradition testify to the search of the Rishis and sages for higher knowledge (para vidya), and their discoveries have been continuously transmitted to posterity and kept alive through its long history, marked by periods of expansion, specialization, decline and renewal. This theme of higher knowledge informs and inspires even the latest developments in the Indian educational system. It has been a significant component of the country's struggle for freedom, attainment of independence and an awakening from the slumber in which people were cast during the British rule.

Despite serious handicaps of means and resources, the country has built up during the last 50 years a very large system of education and has created a vast body of men and women equipped with a high order of scientific and technological capabilities, robust humanist and philosophical thought, and creativity. Though riddled with explosion in the growth of population, a large illiterate population and problems of economic poverty affecting one-third of the people, modern India is still set to forge a bright future and to contribute significantly to the higher goals of world peace, human unity and universal welfare. Much credit for this goes to the ancient but ever-young spirit of the nation and to what higher education has striven to fashion in terms of determining great objectives and implementing them under very difficult conditions.

GROWTH OF HIGHER EDUCATION

Prior to independence, the growth of institutions of higher education in India was very slow and diversification in areas of studies was very limited. After independence, the number of institutions has increased significantly. There are today, 214 universities and equivalent institutions including 116 general universities, 12 science and technology universities, 7 open universities, 33 agricultural universities, 5 women's universities, 11 language universities, and 11 medical universities. Besides, there are universities focusing on journalism, law, fine arts, social work, planning and architecture and other specialized studies. In addition, there are 9703 colleges where 80% of undergraduate and 50% of postgraduate education is imparted. The number of students has reached the level of 6.75 million and there are 3,21,000 teachers in the higher education system.

The government expenditure alone was of the order of Rs. 42,126 millions in 1996-97, and during the subsequent period this has risen even higher. A special emphasis has come to be laid on women's education. The number of women's colleges has recorded a substantial increase, and India has 1195 women's colleges today. The enrolment of women at the beginning of 1997-98 was 2.303 million, 34 per cent of them being of the postgraduate level. This massive development has been guided by a process of planning and recommendations of several national commissions set up by the Government of India.

The objectives of higher education have gradually become more and more precise and a system of governance is developing in the direction of increasing autonomy and accountability. But, in spite of vast efforts over the last 50 years, it is only now that the country is slowly emerging out of the fetters of old ideas and rigid structures, built during the colonial rule. There is at present a demand for radical changes which have the potential to actualise a national system of education that was visualised during the freedom struggle.

Pursuit of integral knowledge and liberation, which has been a constant endeavour of Indian culture, is also the central objective of education. Education is also visualised as an evolutionary force so that each individual is enabled to evolve from purely material consciousness towards superior planes of intellectual and spiritual consciousness. Education is also perceived as a bridge between the past, present, and the future and as a means by which the best of the heritage is transmitted to the new generations for its further progression. In receiving the modern message of learning to be, our endeavour is to harmonise it with the insight of our ancient Indian wisdom according to which this goal can be achieved only by the realisation of our internal and imperishable being.

Our educational system also aims at promoting environmental protection, universal peace, and international cooperation; and since harmony and unity in external space can best be realised through internal purification and perfection, our educational system endeavours to promote harmonious relationship between both the inner and outer dimensions of the individual, environment and the cosmos. Our objective in higher education is not only to promote equality and social justice, but also to provide the right kind of work ethos, professional expertise and leadership in all walks of life. Above all, our endeavour is to foster among teachers and students and, through them in society generally, integral development of values inherent in physical, emotional, rational, aesthetic, ethical and spiritual education.

Structure and System of Governance

In order to implement these objectives, a complex structure and system of governance has been evolving. The structure of higher education consists of three years of education (after 12 years of school education) leading to a bachelor's degree in arts and science and four years in professional fields like engineering and medicine. This is followed by two years of study for a Master's degree; and three years at least beyond the Master's degree for a Ph.D degree which generally takes longer. There are also postgraduate diploma programmes open to graduates, and certain professional programmes like those in education and law require a first degree as a pre-condition for admission in most places.

The universities are of various kinds: with a single faculty, or multi-faculties; teaching or affiliating, or teaching-cum-affiliating, single campus or multi-campus. Most of the universities are "affiliating universities", which prescribe to the affiliated colleges the courses of study, hold examinations and award degrees, while undergraduate and, to some extent, postgraduate instruction is imparted by the colleges affiliated to them. Universities impart postgraduate education and conduct and promote research in a variety of disciplines. Colleges in India are established by State Governments and private agencies. In some cases, universities themselves establish colleges. Most of the colleges seek support from the State Governments for their maintenance. Universities have been set up by the Central or State Governments by means of legislation.

Under the Constitutional scheme, "education" is in the concurrent list, and the Union Government and States exercise joint responsibilities. As a result, while the role and responsibilities of the States in regard to education remains unaltered, the Union Government accepts a larger responsibility to reinforce the national and integrated character of education, to maintain quality and standards, to study and monitor the educational requirements of the country as a whole in regard to manpower for development, to cater to the needs of research and advanced study, to look after international aspects of education, culture and human resource development, and in general, to promote excellence at the tertiary level of the educational pyramid throughout the country. The coordination and cooperation between the Union and the States is brought about in the field of education through the Central Advisory Board of Education (CABE). This body needs strengthening.

In order to determine and maintain standards in universities, the University Grants Commission (UGC) was established in 1952 and was constituted as a statutory body under the Act of Parliament in 1956. In performing its basic functions, the UGC allocates and disburses grants placed at its disposal by the Central Government to the universities, after an assessment of their needs. The Commission provides development and maintenance grants to universities established by the Central Government and provides development grants to the other universities established by the State Governments.

Autonomous colleges

Apart from these initiatives, a number of regulatory measures have been taken to bring about structural reforms and ensure quality in higher education. A scheme of autonomous colleges has been launched under which teachers in the colleges themselves prescribe the curriculum and conduct the evaluation of their students through a system of continuous evaluation. At present, there are 119 autonomous colleges. The UGC constitutes review committees in order to oversee and assess the quality of the university programmes. The UGC and the Council of Scientific and Industrial Research have also set up the National Educational Testing Programmes. UGC has also set up a national level institution for quality assessment and accreditation.

There is also a programme for reforms in the examination system, and various experiments have been conducted to ensure that students are freed from the burden of annual examinations and are encouraged to continue to study throughout the entire period of study. Further thought is being given to broaden these experiments.

Investment in Higher Education

Higher education in India is in deep financial strain, with escalating costs and increasing needs, on the one hand, and shrinking budgetary resources, on the other. The share of higher education in total planned resources increased from 0.71% in the first Five-Year plan to 1.24 % in the fourth Five-Year plan. But ever since, it has declined continuously to 0.53% in the seventh Five-Year plan and further down to 0.35% in the eighth Five-Year plan (1992-97), though the actual expenditure has increased by more than 100 times from Rs.140 million in the first Five-Year plan to Rs. 15,000 million in the eighth Five-Year plan at current prices, and 6.5 times in terms of real prices. Thus, although higher education in India is characterized by massive public investment, this investment is still regarded as much below the optimum.

Recently, major efforts have been mounted for mobilization of resources and it has been recommended that while the Government should make a firm commitment to higher education, institutions of higher education should make efforts to raise their own resources by raising the fee levels, encouraging private donations and by generating revenues through consultancy and other activities. A suggestion has also been mooted for levying an educational cess. It is clearly seen that if higher education has to be maintained and developed further, the Government will have to step up measures for encouraging self-reliance while providing a much more massive investment than hitherto. India, like other countries, visualizes that a new age is dawning, that will be characterised by unimaginable advances in knowledge and synthesis of knowledge, triggering major changes in the objectives, contents, and methods of higher education.

Great emphasis will fall upon lifelong education and the realization of a learning society. Complete education for the complete human personality will come to be emphasized more and more imperatively. Building up the defences of peace in the minds of men and women will continue to make tremendous demands on all levels of education, and higher education will have to bear the responsibility. India also visualizes that contemporary problems can be resolved only if human nature is so changed that mutual goodwill and spontaneous drive to cooperation become ingrained in the human consciousness. India, therefore, visualizes a number of tasks that relate to the creation of a new society that is non-exploitative and non-violent in character by virtue of the integrated personalities of the constituents.

India looks upon the present difficult situation of humanity with realistic optimism. While it is aware of the tremendous dangers that threaten the human aspiration for its higher fulfilment in terms of lasting peace, unity and upliftment of all, it is confident that humanity has the habit of survival and arrival and that it would overcome its pressing problems, even though they require more strenuous and widespread efforts. India is, therefore, preparing itself to join the entire forward looking humanity in its journey to step up the pace in the task of addressing the needs of young people and their future.

OBJECTIVES OF HIGHER EDUCATION IN A CHANGING WORLD

Addressing the graduates of the Allahabad University in 1947, Jawaharlal Nehru, the first Prime Minister of India, said:

> "A university stands for humanism, for tolerance, for reason, for the adventure of ideas and for the search for truth. It stands for the onward march of the human race toward higher objectives. Universities are places of ideals and idealism. If the universities discharge their duties adequately, then, it is well with the nation and the people."

This statement effectively initiated the formulation of the essential purpose of university education in independent India. Universities in India have been the living repository of a long-cherished heritage - a heritage continually revitalised by the teachers and researchers by their contribution to and interaction with it. The higher education system in India has constantly striven to build universities as places of culture and of learning open to all and, above all, reinforcing the theme of learning throughout life. Participating in and contributing to major debates concerning the direction and future of society is seen as a major task, and a moral obligation as well, of the university system.

The first major step taken by the Ministry of Education after independence in higher education was to appoint a Commission on university education under the Chairmanship of Dr. S. Radhakrishnan to report on Indian university education. In its report, the Commission said: "Democracy depends for its very life on a high standard of general, vocational and professional education. Dissemination of learning, incessant search for new knowledge, unceasing effort to plumb the meaning of life, provision for professional education to satisfy the occupational needs of our society are the vital tasks of higher education.

The Commission set out the aims of university education in the following terms:

— Higher education policies and programmes should be in line with the social purposes which we profess to serve;

— There should be a sufficient unity of purpose in the diversity to produce a community of values and ideas among educated men and women;

— Institutional forms may vary as time and circumstances require, but there should be a steadfast loyalty to the abiding elements of respect for human personality, freedom of belief and expression for all citizens, a deep obligation to promote human well-being, faith in reason and humanity;

— Mere vocational and technical education, important though they are, do not necessarily serve the spirit. We might have a number of scientists without conscience and technicians without taste who would find a void, a moral vacuum, within themselves;

— We should preserve the values of democracy, justice and liberty, equality and fraternity. Universities must stand for these ideals which can never be lost so long as men seek wisdom and follow righteousness;

— The Indian Constitution lays down the general purposes of the State. The universities should educate people on the right lines to make the understanding and vision of the framers of the Constitution, the common possession of all the Indian people.

In 1964, the Ministry of Education, Government of India, appointed a Commission to advise the Government on the national pattern of education and on the general principles and policies for the development of education at all stages and in all aspects. In its comprehensive Report, the Commission proposed that education should:

— address the problems of national development, particularly issues concerning self-reliance, economic growth, employment and social and national integration;

— relate to the life, needs and aspirations of the people;

— help improve productivity by emphasi-sing work-experience, vocationalisation, improvements in scientific and technological education and research;

— be perceived as the main instrument of change through human development;

— contribute to social and national integration;

— modernise the society through knowledge and its applications;

— inculcate social, moral and spiritual values in the people.

The Education Commission said in its report:

> "While the fundamental values to which the universities owe their allegiance are largely unrelated to time and circumstances, their functions change from time to time. Their tasks are no longer confined to the two traditional functions of teaching and advancement of knowledge. They are assuming new functions and the older ones are increasing in range, depth and complexity."

The Commission set out the following functions of the universities in the modern world:

— To seek and cultivate new knowledge, to engage vigorously and fearlessly in the pursuit of truth and to interpret old knowledge and beliefs in the light of new needs and discoveries;

— To provide the right kind of leadership in all walks of life by helping the individuals develop their potential;

— To provide society with competent men and women trained in all professions who, as cultivated individuals, are inclined with a sense of social purpose;

— To strive to promote equality and social justice and to reduce social and cultural differences through diffusion of education;

— To foster in the teachers and students, and through them in the society generally, the attitudes and values needed for developing the 'good life' in individuals and society;

— To bring the universities closer to the community through extension of knowledge and its applications for problem-solving.

NATIONAL POLICY ON EDUCATION

Two decades later, the Government of India undertook a comprehensive review of the nation's education policy. The policy statement which emerged following this review reaffirmed: "Education is a unique investment in the present and the future.

This cardinal principle is the key to the National Policy on Education." Higher education, according to the 1986 Policy, provides people with an opportunity to reflect on the critical social, economic, cultural, moral and spiritual issues facing humanity. It contributes to national development through dissemination of specialised knowledge and skills. It is, therefore, a crucial factor for survival. Being at the apex of the educational pyramid, it has also a key role in producing teachers for the education system.

The policy urged that in the context of the unprecedented explosion of knowledge, higher education had to become dynamic as never before, constantly entering uncharted areas, and it proposed that the large number of universities and colleges in the country needed all-round improvement and that the main emphasis in the immediate future should be on their consolidation and expansion. The 1986 policy called for launching the open university system as an instrument of democratising education and to develop a new pattern of the Rural Universities to take up the challenges of micro-planning at grass-root levels for the transformation of the rural areas.

There has recently been a new tide of educational thought which aims at drawing from our current experience of all that is quintessential, as also to develop a new vision in the light of the highest traditions of Indian education and of the contemporary needs and aspirations. The following educational objectives are being emphasised:

— Education aims at liberation - liberation from bondage and ignorance, backwardness and gravitational pulls of the lower human nature;

— Education, being an evolutionary force that enables both the individual and the collectivity to evolve various faculties and to integrate them by the superior intellectual, ethical, aesthetic and spiritual powers, should aim at developing a new type of humanity highly humane, cultured and integrated.

— Education should be developed as a harmonising force, which tries to relate the individual, environment and cosmos in a total harmony by the purification and cultivation of various domains of outer space and inner space;

— Education should be so designed as to become a powerful carrier of the best of the heritage and it should, therefore, aim at transmitting to the new generations the lessons of the accumulated experiences of the past for further progress in the present and the future.

Considering that the contemporary problems of environment, of conflicts and of asymmetrical relationships need to be resolved as early as possible, the Indian system of education aims at the promotion of the goals of universal peace, harmony and unity, based on the principles of liberty, equality and fraternity. Within the broad canvas of these objectives, the specific objectives of higher education that are evolving are:

— To seek and cultivate new knowledge, to engage vigorously and fearlessly in the pursuit of truth, and to interpret all knowledge and beliefs in the light of new things and discoveries;

— To provide the right kind of work ethos, professional expertise and leadership in all walks of life;

— To strive and promote quality and social justice;

— To foster among teachers and students and, through them in society generally, integral development of values inherent in physical, emotional, rational, aesthetic, ethical and spiritual education; and

— To promote synthesis of knowledge, with special emphasis on unity of scientific and spiritual pursuits that would revitalise our country's heritage and promote the ideal of the whole world as one united family.

The theme of higher knowledge and higher education was fashioned in India by the ancient Rishis and sages in the Vedic Age, the date of which is uncertain but is supposed to be traceable to great antiquity. The early Gurukul system of education flourished in the Vedic and Upanishadic periods, but a huge University came to be set up at Takshashila in the 6th Century B.C. Two other universities, namely, Nalanda and Vikramsila were established in the 4th and 5th centuries A.D., respectively. India has had a long tradition of inquiry and articulation of concepts of universe, self, role of state, economy, social order and other related matters. The methodologies adopted were both subjective and objective and included observation, conceptualisation, verification, articulation and teaching.

As a result, India had gone further in science than any other country before the modern era- specially in mathematics, astronomy and chemistry, metallurgy and physics. Indian scientists discovered and formulated and anticipated by force of reasoning or experiment some of the scientific ideas and discoveries which Europe arrived at much later. Ancient India was well equipped in surgery and its system of medicine survives to this day. A vast literature is also available on "Vriksha Ayurveda" (Herbal Medicine). In literature, in philosophy and in systems of yogic knowledge not only ancient India but medieval and modern India reached highest levels of achievement. The higher education system flourished in ancient India well; and it continued to influence developments during its subsequent ages, in spite of diverse forms that developed under the impact of changes in religion, and in social, economic and political life.

MODERN HIGHER EDUCATION

The modern higher education system is only 140 years old, when the first three universities were set up in 1857 under the British Rule. Policy guidelines given by Macaulay and Wood's Despatch shaped the scope and the role of universities in India. To begin with, colleges set up in India were affiliated to British universities. In 1857, for the first time, universities were set up in India. Existing colleges got affiliated to these universities. The period 1857 to 1947 was the period of slow development of institutions of higher education in India. They were set up mostly in administrative headquarters and port towns. They provided education in literature, history, philosophy, political science, social science and natural sciences.

The thrust of development was mainly on liberal arts education. Science education occupied a very small proportion. The rate of development was slow as in a period of 90 years only 18 universities were set up in the country. Most of these followed the model of the three leading universities at Bombay, Calcutta and Madras. Along with liberal arts, some engineering and medical colleges were also set up. Most of the colleges imparted education as formulated by the universities. The universities also acted as examining and degree granting bodies. The initiative in the hands of college teachers in terms of curriculum development was, therefore, very much limited.

The guiding principles of colonial rulers were slightly modified by Indian scholars who desired to blend Indian culture with western thought. They felt this would make Indians appreciate knowledge both from Indian as well as from the British point of view. These two philosophical approaches simultaneously operated during the colonial period. But the development that followed was greatly influenced by Macaulay's Minutes, which had crippling effects, and even till today those effects continue to obstruct the process of major reforms that are now felt to be urgent and imperative.

During this colonial period, particularly after 1906, the desire for a national system of education and need for imparting knowledge of India's philosophy, art and literature also gained momentum. Some of the leading persons attempted to establish indigenous educational institutions with the support of the community. A National College was set up by nationalist leaders in 1906 at Calcutta under the principalship of Sri Aurobindo, and some other institutions too came to be established, such as Viswa Bharati by the great poet Rabindra Nath Tagore.

After independence, India adopted the approach of planned development of the country. The First Five Year Plan focused on agriculture, the Second Five Year Plan on industry and the Third Five Year Plan again attempted to focus on agriculture and agro-based industry for the development of the country. This approach for development called for development of the education system in the subsequent Five Year Plans, to meet the challenges of development and the needs of agriculture, industry and society in general. At Independence in 1947, India inherited a system of higher education which was not only small but also characterized by the persistence of large intra/inter-regional imbalances.

Determined efforts were made to build a network of universities, and their affiliated colleges which provided tremendous outreach to a country of vast diversities in language as also in the prevailing standards of education at the lower levels. The feeder schools differentially impacted on the higher education system leading to significant qualitative imbalances within it. When India became independent, it had only 20 universities and 500 colleges located in different parts of the country. It enrolled around a hundred thousand students in higher education. Participation of women was limited and those who graduated annually were no more than a couple of dozens or so.

The policies and aspirations of people influenced the development in the following decades. In the post-independence period, higher education has expanded fast, and it is mostly public in nature. Today, India ranks very high in terms of the size of the network of higher education institutions, with 6.75 million students enrolled. The teaching force numbers about 321,000. Student enrolment increased from 263,000 to 6,755,000 by 1996-97. It grew at an estimated rate of 7 per cent between 1987 and 1993 but has now declined to 5.5 per cent compound rate of growth, with 14 states (out of 23 States and 1 Union Territory in India which have Universities) having a lower rate.

In spite of this phenomenal growth, the total enrolment, however, forms only about six percent of the relevant age-group (17-23) population. The number of students per 100,000 population has increased significantly since independence. It was only 48 per 100,000 in 1951 increasing to 613 per 100,000 in 1997. India's higher education system compares favourably with the other countries of South Asia and Africa in its enrolment, while our South East Asian neighbours show much higher enrolment such as in the Philippines (27.8%), Thailand (19.0%), and Malaysia (10.1%). Hence, in spite of the rapid expansion of the system in 50 years, access to higher education still remains an issue as the pressure of India's very youthful population continues to bear on it.

With this scientific and technical manpower India has the potential to become the largest reservoir in the world. Compared to the situation that the country inherited from the colonial rulers about half a century ago, these numbers mark a phenomenal expansion of the system.

Table 1. Growth in Higher Education in India

Institutions	1950-51	1990-91	1996-97
Universities	30	117	214
Colleges	750	7346	9703
Enrolment('000s)	263	4925	6755
Teachers('000s)	24.0	272.7	321

The number of women's colleges has recorded a substantial increase from 780 colleges in 1986-87 reaching a figure of 1195 in 1996-97. Of the total enrolment, women's enrolment accounts for 34 per cent. There is a system of National Level Eligibility Test for appointment as teachers in the system. Some States also conduct State Level Tests for appointment of teachers in their States. Positions of Professors and Readers in the Universities are filled through open selection. Under the Career Advancement Scheme, teachers are also promoted to higher positions up to Professors in the Universities and up to Readers in the Colleges. Out of the total number of teachers in higher education, Professors and Readers account for 12.8 and 26.2 per cent respectively, in the University Departments and University Colleges.

In the Affiliated Colleges there are 13.9 per cent Senior Teachers and 81.7 per cent Lecturers. There were 21 students for one teacher in 1996-97 as compared to 12 students per teacher in 1965-66. As a system expands, it absorbs a population of students who come from a wide spectrum of socio-economic groups. The "massification of education" has occurred in India at the lower levels of education which feed into higher education. The quality of that education impacts on higher education. Inevitably, therefore, the higher education system has had to cope with the problems of a very diversified student body from first generation learners to those from professional and higher income families whose children are exposed to many other opportunities besides education.

The first generation learners have mostly attended the publicly funded schools with far poorer preparation than the latter who patronise the private institutions. Increasing access and decrease in quality have been major issues confronting higher education with a very large young population and increasing strain in government resources. Education can have a great role to play in decreasing social disparities between groups and in promoting social mobility. For instance, the tremendous expansion of the middle class in India can be confidently attributed to the investment in education, especially in higher education.

In this respect, the Indian ethos is echoed now in the Delors Report. There is a need to place greater emphasis on enrolment of students from underprivileged backgrounds such as the rural areas, the scheduled castes and tribes and other backward groups, minorities, the disabled and others who have suffered from discrimination which has existed for centuries.

Hence, special attention has to be given to all these groups through various strategies to be adopted in the university system, especially for access to the system, retention in the system and qualitative development of performance.

There are today, 214 universities and equivalent institutions. The total number of universities include six open universities-one central university and five state universities-all run by the government. They also include four universities exclusively meant for women, while all other institutions are open to both males and females. There is no university exclusively for males. Similarly, there are nearly a thousand colleges in the country which give admission exclusively to women students. In addition to providing most of the courses available in other institutions, these colleges and universities provide a few additional courses which are of special interest to women.

Apart from degree awarding university level institutions, there are 9,703 colleges that provide mostly bachelor's and some times master's level education. A majority of the colleges are arts, science and commerce colleges, offering education in humanities, natural sciences, arts and commerce. There are about 550 engineering and technical colleges, 655 medical colleges, nearly 600 management institutions, 700 teacher education/training colleges and 1100 polytechnics. While many universities in India provide general as well as professional education, there are some universities which exclusively provide professional education, and some exclusively general.

Most of the higher education institutions in India are public institutions. There are no private universities so far, though efforts have been initiated to allow opening of private universities. There are, however, a large number of private colleges. A majority of the private colleges are financially supported by the State. The rapid growth of self-financing private colleges is a recent phenomenon.

Governance and Management

Significant progress has been made in recent years not only in the development and strengthening of higher education in terms of improved student access, strengthened research and postgraduate programmes, more equitable representation of different social groups, renewed curricula and adoption of new teaching and delivery methods, but in enhanced institutional management and strategic planning capacity as well. The higher education system has been experimenting with management approaches to deal with challenges arising from internet factors, such as changes in academic disciplines and new instructional methods, and external factors such as population growth, diverse clienteles and changing labour market requirements.

Non-university institutions and establishment of open universities and distance learning system have been particularly important initiatives. Involvement in decision-making by all key stakeholders of higher education institutions is recognised as imperative. To this end, a large measure of autonomy is being stimulated in the system to encourage freedom to select staff and students, determine curriculum and degree standards and to allocate funds; while at the same time being accountable to the system. Higher education in India is coordinated by several agencies. While the university system falls within the jurisdiction of the UGC, professional institutions are coordinated by different bodies.

The All India Council for Technical Education (AICTE) is responsible for coordination of technical and management education institutions. The other statutory bodies are Medical Council of India (MCI), Central Council of Indian Medicine, the Homeopathy Central Council, the Indian Council of Medical Research (ICMR), Indian Nursing Council, the Dental Council, the Pharmacy Council, the Bar Council of India, the Indian Council of Agricultural Research (ICAR), etc. There are also bodies at the state level, such as State Councils of Higher Education that were established recently. There is yet another type of coordinating agency called Association of Indian Universities (AIU), which was earlier known as Inter-University Board of India.

All the universities and other equivalent institutions of higher education are members of the AIU. The AIU has no executive powers, but plays an important role as an agency of dissemination of information and as an advisor both to the government and/or UGC and universities.

The University Grants Commission (UGC)

The University Grants Commission (UGC) was established in 1952 and was constituted as a statutory body under an Act of Parliament in 1956. The establishment of the UGC was the first major legislative measure initiated by the Government of India (GOI) under the constitutional provision reserving to it the powers for coordination and determination of standards in universities. The primary responsibility of the Commission is to promote and coordinate university education in the country and to ensure that the standards are maintained in teaching, research and examinations. In performing these functions, the UGC allocates and disburses grants placed at its disposal by the Central Government to the Universities, after an assessment of their needs.

The Commission provides the development and maintenance grants to universities established under the Acts of Parliament and only development grants to those established by state legislatures. The major initiatives taken by the UGC in improving the quality and standards of higher education are :

- Improvements in the quality and standards of teaching and research through programmes for setting up Centres of Advanced Study and Research, improve-ments in college teaching, strengthening research and infrastructure, etc.
- Periodic review and renewal of curricular content of courses in various disciplines, and special schemes for introduction of emerging areas of education and training.

- — Establishment of common facilities for research networking of resources for information and documentation.
- — Induction of electronic media in higher education.
- — Provision of scholarships and fellowships to students.
- — Launching of special programmes for greater participation of women, disadvantaged groups and the weaker sections in higher education.

All India Council for Technical Education (AICTE)

The AICTE was set up in 1948 as an advisory body to assist the Central Government in the planning and development of technical education at the post-secondary level. Education in engineering and technology, architecture, management and pharmacy is within the purview of the AICTE. In 1988, the AICTE was constituted as a statutory body under an Act of Parliament. The major function of the AICTE is the planned and coordinated development of technical education in the country. In the performance of its functions, the AICTE works in close coordination with the UGC as far as technical education programmes offered by the Universities are concerned.

The AICTE coordinates and supports the development of engineering colleges, management education institutions and polytechnics engaged in the training of technicians. Development support is provided by the AICTE to universities (through the UGC) and engineering colleges and polytechnics for their expansion, as also for improvements in their quality and standards. Among the major programmes supported by the AICTE are review and renewal of the curriculum for the education and training of engineers and technicians. Modernisation of the laboratories and workshops, removal of obsolescence, establishment of community polytechnics, technology forecasting, manpower planning, training of teachers, preparation of norms and standards for programmes of education and training in various disciplines at different levels, and extending the benefits of technical and training to the backward and rural areas.

A significant feature in the development of technical education in the last two decades or so is the emergence of "self-financing" institutions in the private sector which do not depend on government grants, but recover their costs from students in the form of fees. Some of these institutions had their origin in what was then known as "capitation fee" institutions which were set up by private agencies in response to the increasing social demand for professional and technical education, especially in medicine and engineering. Most of them were charging exorbitant fees, and the facilities provided, in many cases, were much below the essential requirements. The Central and State Governments discourage this trend, and legislative measures are being envisaged to regulate the levels of fees that could be charged. There have also been legislations, and the Supreme Court, dealing with a number of cases on the subject, has directed that the Government and its agencies should lay down the principles on the basis of which institutions could levy fees.

National Council for Teacher Education

The National Council for Teacher Education (NCTE) was set up in 1973 by a Government Resolution as a national expert body to advise Central and State Governments on all matters pertaining to teacher education. The Council was made a statutory body by an Act of Parliament in 1993. The primary function of the Council is to ensure planned and coordinated develop-ment of teacher education and determination and maintenance of its standards. For the performance of this function, the Council lays down norms for specified categories of courses and guidelines for granting recognition to teacher training programmes offered by various institutions including universities and colleges.

Indian Council of Agricultural Research

The Indian Council of Agricultural Research (ICAR) was established through a Government Resolution for promotion of agricultural education and research in the country. The council functions under the supervision of the Ministry of Agriculture. Under the auspices of the Council, a number of research institutions and Agricultural Universities have been set up in the country. The ICAR provides funds to these institutions for their development.

In order to ensure a measure of accountability and to evaluate the performance of institutions on the basis of objective criteria, a system of accreditation of institutions of higher learning has been under discussion following the 1986 Policy statement. As far as universities are concerned, the UGC took the initiative and established a mechanism called National Accreditation and Assessment Council (NAAC) as an autonomous council under the aegis of the UGC to carry out periodical assessment of universities and colleges in the country. The methodology developed by NAAC for assessment involves :

— a self-appraisal by each university/college on the basis of specified parameters and documenting its performance with reference to each of them;

— an assessment of the performance by an Expert Committee on the basis of probes identified in respect of each parameter;

— a peer review of the self-appraisal and expert's evaluation; and

— a judgement of the performance.

The NAAC has developed the instruments for carrying out the evaluation studies and several universities and colleges have offered themselves for this assessment. This council needs to be strengthened. The AICTE Act of 1988 envisages the establishment of accreditation mechanisms for institutions offering technical education programmes. The AICTE has since established a National Board of Accreditation (NBA) to initiate the accreditation of technical institutions. As a first step, the NBA has undertaken a detailed exercise for benchmarking the performance of premier institutions so that a frame of reference for the evaluation of the performance of the institutions can be initiated.

The University System

The universities are of various kinds: with a single faculty or many faculties; teaching or affiliating, or teaching-cum-affiliating; single-campus or multi-campus; Agricultural Universities; Medical Universities; Tech-nological Universities; Language Universities (Hindi, Sanskrit, Tamil, Telugu, Urdu); and Women's Universities. There are besides special institutions in medicine, science, engineering and technology, management and social sciences. All these institutions of higher learning can be classified into the following categories:

— Universities which are established by an Act of Parliament or State Legislature and are of unitary or affiliating type;

— Institutions of national importance - such as the Indian Institutes of Technology - which are established under Acts of Parliament and are empowered to award degrees.

— Institutions deemed to be universities, which are given university status under a provision in the UGC Act. Some of these institutions offer advance level courses in a particular field of specialisa-tion, while many of them award general degrees.

— Institutions which award only diplomas and are not established by legislation or not declared as deemed to be universities. The Indian Institutes of Management are in this category.

The UGC Act has a provision which prohibits any institution from awarding degrees unless it is established under an act of

Parliament or a State Legislature, or is specially empowered to award degrees through legislation, or is deemed to be a university under the UGC Act. The first institution to be given the status of a university was Serampore College, near Calcutta, in 1829. The first three universities established in India in 1857 at Calcutta, Bombay and Madras were "affiliating universities" following the model of the London University. Later, Allahabad University, which has completed one hundred years, was established as a unitary university. In this dispensation, the universities prescribed the courses of study, held examinations and awarded degrees, while all instruction was imparted by the colleges.

It was only during the period between 1904 and 1913 that imparting instruction within the universities began in India. Even so, the gene- ral pattern of affiliation of colleges continues with most of the universities in the country. Since the colleges do not have the power to award degrees, they have necessarily to seek affiliation from a university. As the number of universities multiplied, and most of them sought to cater to the needs of a region or a state, a system of jurisdiction over specified territories among the universities, for the purpose of affiliation of colleges, also evolved. The power of granting affiliation to a college is vested in the universities. Most universities have laid down detailed conditions which the management of a college has to fulfil before its application for affiliation is considered by the university.

Most universities insist on physical inspection before taking any decision on affiliation. In an attempt to ensure the process of affiliation on a more rigorous academic exercise, the UGC has recommended detailed guidelines to all the universities in the country. Colleges in India are established by the state governments and private agencies. In some cases, the universities themselves establish colleges. Although the number of colleges established under private initiative is fairly large, more often, most of them begin to seek support from the state governments for their maintenance.

Today, most of the colleges, with the exception of those which are self-financing, are receiving financial support from public funds. Although there is a broad consensus on the core issues of university management, on matters of detail, perceptions and views vary. The core issues on which there is a broad consensus are:

— Universities management should be structured on the principle of self-governance based on participation, decentralisation, autonomy and accountability;

— The various constituents of a university, namely, Faculties, Schools, Departments, Colleges, etc., should have the freedom to achieve excellence; and

— The main Act of a University should lay down the structure and organisation in broad terms and the relevant details may be prescribed by statutes and ordinances.

The collegiate landscape is a wide, heterogeneous spectrum of institutions and services. The pattern of governance varies considerably in terms of their internal administration as well as in their relationship with their external environment, the major constituents of which are the university and the government. The universities have to ensure the maintenance of academic standards in their affiliated colleges, and the state governments meet part or whole of the expenditure incurred by these institutions; other issues that relate to staff and students and their roles in the organisation, administration and development of their campuses are largely left to the resourcefulness of individual colleges.

Instruction for almost 80% of the enrolment in first degree programmes is imparted in colleges. Since the universities concerned prescribe the courses, set the standards and conduct the examinations, the large body of college teachers are left with very little option in deciding what to teach and how. The UGC has, therefore, evolved a scheme to confer autonomous status on selected colleges which would enable them to prescribe the courses, determine the content and decide the teaching-learning processes. The colleges would continue to remain affiliated to the universities whose major functions would be to approve the courses, hold the examinations and award the degrees.

The experiment has led to the review and renewal of the curricular content of the programmes offered by the autonomous colleges, and imparting to the programmes some measure of relevance. Universities are creations of legislatures and they are by and large financed from public funds. They have therefore to be accountable to the concerned legislatures and governments. Performance of the functions, which require exercise of academic judgement lies exclusively within the domain of universities. A new awareness is growing that while the status of teachers should be raised, there should also be a corresponding system of their accountability.

There are, at the national level, a multiplicity of Councils established by the Government of India as statutory mechanisms for developing and regulating various professions. To the extent the preparation for all these professions is done by the universities through education and training, they have to satisfy the regulator's prescriptions of standards of professional preparation, though most of them are not involved in the resource allocation processes. A number of Research Councils have been set up, notable among them being the Indian Council of Philosophical Research, Indian Council of Historical Research, Indian Council of Social Science Research, Indian Institute of Advanced Study, National Council of Rural Institutes, Central Council of Research in Ayurveda and Siddha, Rashtriya Sanskrit Samsthan, and Rashtriya Veda Vidya Pratishthan.

In this age of a techno-scientific revolution, when the sheer quantity of knowledge and information is expanding exponentially, when the needs of a constantly growing and increasingly varied student population are burgeoning, the quality of training for teachers and the quality of teaching in higher education institutions demand top priority. The higher education system in India recognises its key responsibility in training teachers, in establishing links with teacher training institutions at other levels and in training teacher trainers. Efforts are being made to bring in teachers from the commercial and social sectors to facilitate interchange and build links with the education system. The higher education system in India is facilitating access to the common heritage of knowledge and research. It is fulfilling its moral obligation to society in exchange for the resources assigned to it by society.

Recently, a Task Force on Fundamental Duties laid down in the Constitution has been constituted so that the same can be reflected in the curriculum. This would also lay down a code of accountability of all stakeholders in the educational system. The University Grants Commission [UGC] was set up in 1956 as an agency for coordination and maintenance of the standards of teaching examination and research in universities. During the last 40 years, the UGC has taken a number of measures to improve quality and to introduce innovations. Quality improvement through infrastructural development: Here the policy is to ensure a minimum level of facilities such as laboratories, libraries, classrooms and hostels, by the provision of development grants. Special grants have also been provided to improve in quality humanities, social science and science streams.

Financial support has also been provided for creating new inter-disciplinary oriented universities such as the Jawaharlal Nehru University. Curriculum, human resources and research development: Another quality assurance measure is the provision of resources in the form of Research Fellowships for M.Phil. and Ph.D. programmes undertaken by university and college teachers, University leadership programmes (ULP) for college teachers, and Seminars, workshops, summer schools in various subjects so as to help the teachers upgrade their knowledge. Such programmes reach a large number of teachers in the system. In 1987, Academic Staff Colleges (ASC) were set up to provide opportunities for general orientation and subject refresher programmes for academic staff.

Under the scheme, more than hundred thousand teachers have received orientation and subject refresher programmes of 3-4 weeks duration. Such measures are expected to have greater impact on the quality of teaching and learning in the system of higher education in the country. Other measures within this broad category are restructuring of courses, improving the quality of research and curriculum development by constituting various subject panels and encouraging universities to undertake constant revision and improvement of curriculum. In order to implement relevant curricula, a scheme of restructuring of undergraduate programmes was initiated. The scheme envisaged flexible and socially relevant undergraduate curricula with a provision for foundation, core, application and skills-oriented course components.

A recent innovation has been the introduction of the vocational education scheme, at the undergraduate level. Under this scheme one of three subjects required for having a Bachelor's Degree could be a vocational education subject. The scheme has suggested 35 vocational subjects and recently some more vocational subjects related to agriculture and rural areas have been introduced. Nearly 1,500 colleges have been given facilities for vocational education and a large amount has been invested to support the implementation.

Centres of Excellence in Higher Education

Centres of excellence in different subject specialities have been established under the scheme of Centres of Advanced Studies (CAS), Department of Special Assistance (DSA) and Inter-University Research centres at internationally comparable standards. The objectives of these centres are to provide quality input in higher education and in research areas. Great strides in science and technology, on the one hand, and high cost of inputs for good research, on the other, have made it necessary to develop interactive institutional arrangements between teaching institutions, national research laboratories and the development sectors. The UGC has established Inter-University Centres to enable cooperation and joint use of facilities in nuclear science, crystal growth astronomy and astrophysics, social sciences and humanities.

Information Centres to facilitate information flow have been set up at the Indian Institute of Science, Bangalore, M.S. University of Baroda and SNDT Women's University, Bombay. Sudden expansion in the higher education system required the development of excellence. A major strategy has been devised by the UGC for establishing Advanced Centres and Departments of Special Assistance within the university system. At present, about 411 departments are participating in these schemes and 157 in the scheme for strengthening the infrastructure facilities for postgraduates and research in science. These schemes have had a major impact on raising standards and promoting excellence in higher education.

Research is promoted by encouraging students to do M.Phil. and Ph.D. research. The UGC provides financial assistance to those who are meritorious and propose to pursue research. Meritorious students are selected through National Level Test. Nearly 50,000 scholars are receiving Fellowships for conducting research. Those who are enrolled for research programme account for 74,000, i.e. 1.1 per cent of total enrolment in higher education. Nearly 10,000 students are awarded Ph.D. degree every year.

Teachers are encouraged to do research through award of minor and major research projects. Nearly 500 major research projects and 650 minor research projects were awarded during the last year. Besides, there are schemes of Research Associateship, Scientistship, Emeritus Fellowship, Teacher Fellowship and Career Awards through which research work is supported by providing financial assistance to teachers. These Fellowships are available for Science, Social Sciences, Humanities and Engineering & Technology. Besides UGC, support for major and minor research projects is provided to teachers in higher education by Department of Science and Technology and various Councils related to Social sciences, History and Philosophy.

Training of teachers is an important component of any policy, which aims at maintaining high standards of teaching in the universities and colleges. The review of Educational Policy stressed upon a comprehensive programme of professional development of teachers through Academic Staff Colleges. The scheme of Academic Staff Colleges was started in 1986-87, under which 45 such Colleges have been set up so far. These colleges conduct four-week orientation programmes for training new teachers with innovative techniques and also three to four week refresher courses in various disciplines for in-service teachers to enable them to update their knowledge. Since these Academic Staff Colleges cannot cater to the needs of all the teachers, 72 departments of universities and specialised institutions have been selected to conduct refresher courses, in addition to the Academic Staff Colleges.

These centres have prepared reading material for the use of teachers. The Academic Staff Colleges also conduct seminars of two to three days' duration for the Principals located under the catchment area. The Academic Staff Colleges sensitise the teachers about students' expectations and perceptions and provide them an understanding of the academic context of higher education. They also help teachers in developing insights into the dynamics of working in the educational system. Up to 31st March, 1997, nearly 1.14 lakh teachers had participated in refresher courses and 42,000 teachers in orientation courses.

To enrich the quality of higher education, a Country-wide Classroom scheme was launched. Under this scheme, special films on various subjects were prepared and broadcast for the benefit of students and teachers. To carry this out, institutional audio-visual research centres and educational media research centres were set up throughout the country. Such Centres already number 21 and are likely to increase. These centres are producing a large number of video tapes that are transmitted on the national TV network.

The regulatory system was introduced as early as in 1857 along with the establishment of the modern university in India. The main purpose was to ensure the standardisation of curriculum in undergraduate programme, as well as objective and impersonal evaluation of students. The system of affiliated colleges involved determination of curriculum by the university. Implementation of this curriculum was carried out by the affiliated colleges and university departments and evaluation of students through comprehensive examinations. So long as the system remained small in size, it worked reasonably well. But, with the expansion in the number of institutions and students, this system has become counter-productive and has caused serious damage to the process of teaching and learning; diversification of higher education, social relevance of the curriculum and evaluation of students.

In order to remedy this situation, the following steps have been taken:

— *Scheme of Autonomous Colleges*: These are intended to ensure quality relevance and appropriate assessment of students. Under this arrangement, teachers in the colleges decide the curriculum and conduct the evaluation of their students through systems of continuous evaluation. At present, there are 119 autonomous colleges.

— *Critical inputs and recognition*: Other regulatory measures, such as creation of minimum level of infrastructure, the specified number of qualified staff and well-defined administrative procedures, are insisted upon before any institution is affiliated to a university, or before a university can be recognised by the UGC for financial assistance. These measures discourage the opening of substandard institutions.

UGC review committees and visiting committees oversee and assess the quality of university programmes. These committees are constituted for different areas and disciplines and for all the universities which receive financial assistance from the UGC. Another UGC measure is the National Educational Testing (NET) programme. The UGC and the Council of Scientific and Industrial Research (CSIR) conduct tests in science subjects twice a year for Junior Research Fellowships (JRF) and an eligibility test for the teaching profession. Universities and colleges are required to consider the candidature of only such persons who have qualified for teaching jobs. Those who qualify for JRF tests are awarded Junior Research Fellowships of Rs. 5,000/- per month. These tests have proved to be important indicators of quality of students engaged in the teaching and research profession.

As a part of coordination and maintenance of standards of higher education, the UGC has set up an Inter-University Institution of quality assessment and accreditation. This is named as National Assessment and Accreditation Council (NAAC) and it was set up in 1994 under Section 12 CCC of the UGC Act. NAAC's responsibility is to assess and accredit institutions of higher education that volunteer for the process, based on certain criteria which can be applied to the functioning of the institution in totality. NAAC's process of assessment and accreditation involves the preparation of a self-study report by the institution, its validation by the peers and final decision by the Council. Though assessment and accreditation is voluntary on the part of the institutions, UGC has already indicated that its plan-based development support to educational institutions will be related to the outcome of assessment and accreditation.

It has already extended financial support to the extent of Rs. 5 lakhs to each university to meet the expenses involved in undergoing the accreditation process. Likewise, the autonomous colleges are provided with financial support for this purpose as a part their annual grant from the UGC. So far 47 universities, 75 affiliated colleges and 20 autonomous colleges have volunteered to be accredited by NAAC. Around 10 universities and 25 colleges are in the advanced stage of finalising the self-study report in a few months time. The on-site visit to seven institutions - one university and six colleges-has already been completed. For a few more institutions, the on-site visit is being planned.

Open University System

The advances in information and communication technology provide great opportunities to enhance teaching and learning in higher education by both on-campus and distance education. Even disabled students who are denied access to traditional institutions, and all those who require updating of their knowledge and life-long education can now be benefited by the modern facilities of communication. They also provide increased access to information sources and facilitate communication among researchers and teachers and the building of networks of institutions and scholars. Through the open universities and distance learning initiatives, mechanisms are in place to upgrade skills at regular intervals and develop new competencies.

People's needs of lifelong learning are constantly expanding. Higher education institutions are offering learning opportunities to satisfy these diverse demands. Ready access and flexibility are the hallmarks of these initiatives. The Open University System was initiated in the country to augment opportunities for higher education as an instrument of democratising education and also to make it a lifelong process. The first open university in the country was established by the state government of Andhra Pradesh in 1982. In 1985, the central government established the Indira Gandhi National Open University (IGNOU).

Indira Gandhi National Open University

The IGNOU designed, developed and delivered high quality academic programmes in the Humanities, Sciences and Social

Sciences as well as in professional areas like Computer Applications, Education, Engineering, Management, Nursing and Tourism. The University has currently 39 programmes comprising 482 courses to offer. Most of the University's programmes are structured on modular pattern, leading to the award of certificates, diplomas and degrees. The enrolment in the university has been rising rapidly. From less than 4,000 students in 1987, the enrolment rose to over 1,60,000 in 1998. The University has a vastly heterogeneous student body: demographically diverse (age, gender, region, social background, etc.); educationally dis-advantaged (most of them without the traditional qualifications for entering into higher education and who have had no other opportunities to make up for the lost time); and economically weak (large majority belonging to low and lower middle income groups).

Most of these students are in the lower rungs of their career looking for opportunities to improve their qualifications, professional competence and/or in acquiring new skills. The University has demonstrated that modern communication technologies can be effectively harnessed in providing access to educational opportunities and that high technology need not necessarily be a high cost medium. The University has, at its inception, set up Audio-Video production facilities with the generous support provided by the Governments of UK and Japan. These facilities were substantially augmented with a major grant given by the Government of Japan. The current Electronic Media Production Centre is a state-of-the-art technological facility that significantly enriches the university's learning packages. The media packages of the university are transmitted on the nation-wide television network as well as through selected radio stations.

A dedicated, satellite-based teleconferencing network is being developed on an experimental basis in cooperation with the Indian Space Research Organisation for providing interactive teaching- learning support to distance education programmes offered by open universities in India. For the delivery of various services to its students, the IGNOU has developed a nation-wide network of 19 Regional Centres, 334 Study Centres/ programme centres and 40 work centres. The Study Centres and Work Centres are located generally with existing educational or training institutions who have made their facilities and services available to the IGNOU students.

Since the establishment of the IGNOU, seven more open universities were established in different states (Bihar, Gujarat, Karnataka, Madhya Pradesh, Maharashtra, Rajasthan and West Bengal). A few more state governments are considering the establishing of open universities.

Distance Education Council (DEC)

The IGNOU is also a national level apex body for distance education. The apex body role envisages the establishment and development of an Open University Network by sharing the intellectual and physical resources within the distance education system among different institutions and enriching the system by extending its outreach, on the one hand, and ensuring the quality standards of its programmes of education and training, on the other. For the performance of this function, a Distance Education Council has been established as a statutory authority under the IGNOU Act. In discharging its responsibility, the Distance Education Council also provides development funding to open universities and distance education institutions from the funds placed at its disposal by the Central Government.

Open University Network

The Distance Education Council (DEC) has taken several initiatives to develop the Open University Network. A major step taken by the DEC is the establishment of a Common Pool of Programmes, consisting of contributions from different open universities, which can be shared by an Open University through the process of adoption, adaptation and/or translation. The programmes developed and produced by IGNOU are extensively used by the State Open Universities in the country. Efforts have also been made to evolve common standards for the products as well as processes (programme structure, credits, examination, grading, etc.) to facilitate student mobility across programmes as well as institutions through systems of credit transfer. Steps have also been initiated of credit transfer.

Steps have also been initiated to frame norms and standards for the design, development and delivery of programmes in specific fields and to ensure their quality. The Open University programmes have proved to be highly cost-effective. The current indications are that their cost varies between 35 and 50 per cent of the cost normally incurred by the traditional system on comparable programmes. The open universities could bring down this cost further through economies of scale since a part of its fixed cost will get distributed over a larger number of students. The open universities in the country have generally developed their programmes and courses with a view to ensure that they are relevant to the economic and employment needs.

Most of their programmes are very different from those offered by the traditional universities. They are designed and developed in several modules to assist the potential students to choose such modules as they perceive are relevant to their needs. On their part, the universities have also sought to diversify their course provisions and developed high quality multi-media open learning curriculum designed to meet the academic, technical and vocational needs of diverse student groups. A notable feature of these programmes especially those in the technical, vocational and professional areas is the close linkages with the industry and other employer groups, not only in designing and preparing the learning packages, but also in the delivery of various services to the students at the work place. The open university programmes offered by IGNOU have received international attention and recognition.

Financing of Higher Education

Demand for higher educated manpower will increase substantially in the near future and this will impel central focus on the quality and quantity of manpower produced by the higher education system. Both for quantitative expansion and improvement in quality, the system requires large additional resources. Increasing needs stemming from population growth, need for modernisation and the limited nature of resources, are problems facing financing of education. The concept of 'investment in education' was explicitly adopted by the Government of India in the National Policy on Education, 1968. Keeping in view the growing requirements of the education system, the Government of India has promised to allocate at least six per cent of national income to education from the public exchequer. This goal is set for realisation by the end of the ninth Five Year Plan.

Besides its social and cultural dimensions, education is also an economic and political investment yielding long-term benefits. It is, therefore, not only justifiable but desirable to raise money from private sources in order to ease pressure on public spending. This, of course, is not meant to release the state from its financial commitments, which have been substantial in India.

GROWTH IN EXPENDITURE ON HIGHER EDUCATION

Higher education in India is in financial stress. However, it should be noted that huge investments have been made in higher education in independent India. Total expenditure on higher education has increased remarkably during the post-independence period. At the inception of planning in the country (1950-51), India was spending Rs. 172 million on higher education. Government expenditure alone was of the order of Rs. 42,035 million in 1996-97, and it has risen further during the subsequent period. This impressive growth is, however, considerably offset by increase in prices, and increase in population, more particularly student numbers in higher education. Inflation has had an adverse effect on education.

Nevertheless, on the whole, the trends suggest that higher education had a good start during the 1950s (with real growth of 7.5 per cent per annum), and had its golden days during the 1960s, with the real expenditure increasing at an annual rate of growth of 11 per cent; but it suffered significantly during the 1970s, with the rate of growth coming down to a meagre 3.4 per cent as educational planners aimed at consolidation of higher education instead of its rapid expansion; and showed some tendencies to recover during the 1980s. Though the growth in expenditure on higher education has been erratic during the 1980s, it had increased on the whole at a rate of growth of 7.3 per cent per annum. The 1990s heralded an era of austerity and higher education suffered greatly.

The relative priority accorded to higher education can be measured in terms of the share of higher education in GNP. Starting from a very low figure of 0.19 per cent of GNP invested in higher education in 1950-51, the share of higher education increased five-fold by 1980-81; but it came down to nearly one per cent of GNP after three decades of development. But ever since, allocation of resources has been steadily coming down: it tended to decline to 0.4 per cent of GNP by mid 1990s. India has adopted Five Year Plans as an important development strategy since 1950. The Five Year Plans set new directions for development-quantitative expansion, improvement in quality and relating to several other dimensions of education development-and represent the serious intention of the planners to further develop the system.

The share of higher education doubled in the total education outlay from 9 per cent in the first Five Year Plan to 18 per cent in the second Five Year Plan, and increased to an all time peak of 25 per cent in the fourth Five Year Plan, and ever since it has been consistently declining, and was about 15 per cent in the seventh Five Year Plan. The share of higher education in the total education outlay in the eighth Five Year Plan was estimated to be 8 per cent. In case of education, including higher education, plan expenditures are of relatively small size and huge amounts are incurred as 'non-plan expenditures', i.e., for the maintenance of the gigantic system, recognised as the second largest system in the world.

In the total expenditure on education, the share of higher education was less than one-fifth in 1950-51, it increased to about a quarter by 1955-56, and became stable around one-fourth, suggesting that the relative importance given to higher education in the total education system remained unchanged since the beginning of the second Five Year Plan up to the sixth Five Year Plan, though there had been marginal increases during this period. But the situation has changed considerably from the seventh Five Year Plan onwards. Devaluation, and the accompanying price rise, has led to an enormous increase in prices of books and journals; and as a result, many universities have had to inflict very serious cuts on their library budgets.

The various sources of finances for higher education in India are:

(a) government sector - central government, and state government; and

(b) Non-governmental sector- students/parents (or families), e.g., fees, and other maintenance expenditure, and the rest of the community at large, e.g., donations and endowments.

The relative shares of various sources in 'total' expenditure on higher education in India have changed considerably over the years. The share of the government has increased in financing higher education, and correspondingly that of every other source, viz., student fees, community contributions, and other internal sources declined steeply, though in absolute money terms there has been a significant increase in the contribution of these sources as well. The share of government (central and state) increased from 49 per cent in 1950-51 to 76 per cent in 1986-87. And the share of the non-governmental sector declined remarkably. Students' contributions in the form of fees used to form more than one-third of the total until the beginning of the 1960s; its relative share declined to less than half of what it was in 1950-51.

The share of "other" sources (including voluntary donations, endowments, etc.) also declined, though the decline is not as sharp as the decline in the share of the fees. Non-governmental finances (fees and others) accounted for one-fourth of the total. Thus, higher education in India is characterised by massive public investment, though the investment is still regarded as much below optimum. Such a rapid growth in public financing of higher education in India has been necessary for the following reasons:

— Facilities for higher education available at the time of independence were insignificant. Independence had created an abnormal increase in the social demand for higher education, and public expenditure has had to cope with the demand.

— Building up a new socio-economic system after the end of the colonial rule required large scale manpower with varied skills; so the government had to expand investment in higher education.

— The very development models emphasised high skilled labour force, and building up of huge social infrastructure for excellence in science and technology, and research and development.

— Government policies towards equality in education led to the growth in public investment in education, since it involves huge subsidies at all levels of education to a substantial number of students, belonging to weaker sections.

— The rapid growth of school education naturally pushed the demand for higher education.

Recently, efforts are being made to mobilise resources, and it has been recommended that while the government should make a firm commitment of funding higher education, colleges and universities should also make efforts to raise their own resources.

Current Policy Issues in Financing

Generally it is felt that the levels of fees in higher education in India are very low and that there exists much scope for increase in the fee and for rationalisation of the fee structure. This is more so in case of higher technical education. The UGC and AICTE Committees recommended that at least 20 per cent of the recurring expenditure per student has to be generated through student fees (and other sources). Student loan programme has been one of the most prominent methods that is currently suggested as an effective solution to the problem of financing higher education. This is also advocated as an effective antidote to check the regressive effects of increase in fees. Many nationalised banks in India have begun to offer a variety of loans to students for higher education within the country and abroad. An idea has been mooted to levy an educational cess on industries and other organisations that use technical manpower.

Several measures are being suggested for efficient utilisation of resources in educational institutions and to effect economy in expenditures, including the one related to the consolidation of uneconomic institutions. For effective utilisation of available resources, it is necessary that an optimum size of the institutions is worked out. Institutions with small size would be uneconomic and in the institutions with large student numbers, the resources might be over-optimally utilised. The AICTE felt that institutions of technical education should have enrolments in the range of 1,500-2,000, with a minimum annual intake of 180, and with an intake of 40-60 for every course/discipline. The Committee has also suggested staff-student ratios to vary between 1:15 and 1:20. Available data on some engineering institutions show that more than half the institutions were having enrolment below 1,500, and more than 80 per cent of the institutions have a staff-student ratio of less than 1:15. All this suggests the need for consolidation of technical education institutions, through proper institutional planning.

Privatisation of Higher Education

The new trends of thinking and overall constraint in resources call for private initiative and community support. In the Indian mixed economy, while the contribution of private sector has been significant in general, its contribution to higher education has not been encouraging. While until now there is no formal private university in India, there are a large number of private colleges in the general and technical education spheres. Private colleges that form about three-fourths of the total number of colleges, are of two types: privately managed but publicly funded colleges familiarly known as (government) "aided" colleges, and privately managed and funded colleges, known as "unaided" colleges. A substantial number of private colleges belong to the former category, and they receive government aid to meet almost the whole recurrent expenditure.

The private aided colleges have not contributed significantly to easing the financial burden of the government, as more than 95 per cent of the recurring expenditure, and sometimes even the capital expenditure, is met by public exchequer. Hence strictly from the point of view of finances, such private colleges do not have any significant role. Pure or "unaided" private colleges do provide financial relief to the government in providing higher education, but at huge and long-term economic and non-economic cost to the society. Such institutions have been really a recent phenomenon. They are the result of private enterprise and initiative. In the very recent period, growth of private engineering and medical colleges has been remarkable. They charge donations and capitation fees. While other colleges are, by definition, non-profit institutions, many of these institutions not merely cover their costs, but also make profits, which are not necessarily re-invested in education. The government wants to encourage private initiatives in higher education but not commercialisation.

Now-a-days with declining or stagnant budgets for education, specifically for higher education, institutions of higher education increasingly feel the need to become financially self-reliant by generating resources not only through increase in fees, but also through other measures, such as augmentation of resources from corporate sector in the form of donations and other similar contributions, by forging effective relationships with industry. The government has already promised incentives both to the institutions and to the individual donors. The institutions that generate such resources are promised matching grants by the government, besides stating that such resources would not be taken into account in giving bulk/maintenance grants. The donors are offered fiscal incentives in income tax savings (tax deduction at the rate of 125 per cent of the contributions to professional institutions and 100 per cent to other institutions of education). It is, however, recognised that none of these measures for mobilisation of additional resources should aim at reducing the demand for higher education.

NEW CHALLENGES FOR THE HIGHER EDUCATION

India recognises that the new global scenario poses unprecedented challenges for the higher education system. The University Grants Commission has appropriately stated that a whole range of skills will be demanded from the graduates of humanities, social sciences, natural sciences and commerce, as well as from the various professional disciplines such as agriculture, law, management, medicine or engineering. India can no longer continue the model of general education as it has been persisting in for the large bulk of the student population. Rather, it requires a major investment to make human resource productive by coupling the older general disciplines of humanities, social sciences, natural sciences and commerce to their applications in the new economy and having adequate field based experience to enhance knowledge with skills and develop appropriate attitudes.

Responding to these emerging needs, the UGC stated: "The university has a crucial role to play in promoting social change. It must make an impact on the community if it is to retain its legitimacy and gain public support". It seeks to do so by a new emphasis on community based programmes and work on social issues. Concepts of access, equity, relevance and quality can be operationalised only if the system is both effective and efficient. Hence, the management of higher education and the total networking of the system for effective management, has become an important issue. The shift can occur only through a systemic approach to change as also the development of its human resource, and networking the system through information and communi-cation technology. The decline in public funding in the last two plan periods has resulted in serious effects on standards due to increasing costs on non-salary items and emoluments of staff, on the one hand, and declining resources, on the other.

Effective measures will have to be adopted to mobilize resources for higher education. There is also a need to relate the fee structure to the student's capacity to pay for the cost, so that, students at lower economic levels can be given highly subsidised and fully subsidised education. The Ninth Plan policy imperatives will focus on

1. access and equity;
2. relevance and quality of education;
3. universities and social change;
4. the delivery systems, the institutional and organisational structures and management; and

5. funding which constitutes the necessary resource underpinning for development.

Emphasis has to be laid on curriculum change; interdisciplinary courses gradually replacing discipline oriented learning, especially at the master's degree level; greater emphasis on field based learning experiences for students both in undergraduate and postgraduate programmes; more career oriented courses and response to local needs for human resource in specific work-related opportunities. The university is required to be seen not only as a seat of learning and new knowledge through its research and extension functions but also as a focal point for the dissemination of information to the community through continuing education, extension education and through field outreach activities. It will have a major role to play in directly impacting on the community for social development and change. It should be facilitated in this task which is described by the UGC as the third dimension of education.

As universities abandon their isolationist existence and increasingly interact with other segments of society, there is a need for them to adopt a more professional management. This includes opting for a new type of leadership capable of interfacing with user and other groups in society, and at the same time, capable of providing academic and administrative leadership within a decentralised system of administration, and making increased use of information technology. The above implies that there will be greater interaction with the user community of both employers and the public to create relevant programmes, to develop greater autonomy in a decentralised structure and to develop a professional management system which has autonomy as well as accountability, and maximising the use of information technology for both effective and efficient management.

As a very small proportion of the relevant age group (around 6 per cent) is enrolled in higher education in India, compared to the developed countries (about 40%) with which the country is going to engage itself in the international market, efforts will need to be directed towards raising the enrolment in higher education sector and meeting the increasing costs of such enrolment. Access means costs but access cannot be overlooked when the base is narrow, not in absolute numbers but in the percentage of the educated in the country's structure. We have to acknowledge the need to prepare a human resource capable of accepting the challenges of the new millennium.We have also to realise that social changes and transformation can only be brought about by people and not through technology alone which itself is a product of human endeavour. Hence, human resource development, at all levels, needs to be given priority and made a part of the nation's overall strategy.

INTERNATIONAL COOPERATION

Universities in India have been a primary conduit for the advancement and transmission of knowledge through traditional functions such as research, innovation, teaching, human resource development, and continuing education. International cooperation is gaining importance as yet another function. With the increased development of transport and communication, the global village is witnessing a growing emphasis on international cooperation and action to find satisfactory solutions to problems that have global dimensions. And, higher education is one of them. India has been in the forefront to adopt the new 'information society' technologies such as distance education and the internet to forestall the further widening of the gap between itself and the advanced countries. International cooperation in education is seen in this context of partnership - rather than aid - where countries assist each other by sharing their successful experiences, technologies, material and financial resources and learning to appreciate each other's cultural heritage.

International cooperation has also been an important focus area in promoting the ideals and objectives of higher education. The Indian National Commission for Cooperation with

UNESCO (INC), set up in 1949, is an apex advisory, executive, liaison, information and coordinating body at the national level. INC has been playing an active role in UNESCO's work, particularly in the formulation and execution of its programme in collaboration with the UNESCO Secretariat as well as the National Commissions of Asia and the Pacific Region. India contributes to the activities of UNESCO and its Regional Offices through participation in numerous workshops, symposia and conferences, by assisting in the organisation of national, regional and inter-regional activities in India in areas of competence of UNESCO, arranging participation of Indian experts in UNESCO's activities, formulating projects under the Participation Programme of UNESCO and administration of UNESCO Coupons Scheme.

India is a member of the Executive Board of UNESCO. Public information activities relating to UNESCO are supported in the form of publication of Hindi and Tamil editions of the Courier, a UNESCO periodical. So far, nine UNESCO Chairs have been set up in India in diverse areas such as cultural development, eco-technology, science education, peace, human rights and democracy, energy, small industries and teacher education. Proposals for setting up UNESCO Chairs in social economics, biotechnology, social anthropology, medicinal plants and cultural identities are under consideration. The UNITWIN/UNESCO Chairs Programme was launched by UNESCO in 1991 as an international action plan and movement for academic solidarity to strengthen inter-university cooperation, with particular emphasis on support to higher education in the developing countries.

The programme aims at establishing and reinforcing strong and durable links amongst higher education and scientific institutions world-wide. The programme has the following goals:

— to give fresh impetus and a global dimension to twinning and other linking arrangements between higher education institutions in the industrialised and developing countries;

— to reinforce existing sub-regional and inter-regional cooperation networks of higher education and research institutions and to establish new networks, whenever there is a perceived need;

— to develop centres of excellence for specialised studies and advanced research, with international support;

— to alleviate the consequences of the brain drain.

T]he programme focuses on graduate studies and research and places particular emphasis on developing strategies and mechanisms for the rapid and efficient transfer of knowledge and for its application to specific national and local conditions and needs. The INC operates the UNESCO International Coupon Programme which assists individuals and institutions working in the fields of education, science, culture and communication to import their bonafide requirement of educational publications, scientific equipment, educational films, etc., from abroad without undergoing the foreign exchange and import control formalities.

The Department of Education in the Ministry of Human Resource Development has also built relations with other international organisations such as the Commonwealth Secretariat, Commonwealth of Learning, SAARC, UN Organisations and NAM and Shastri Indo-Canadian Institute, etc. The External Academic Unit of the Department handles policy matters to promote India's external academic relations with more than 97 countries with whom India has bilateral Cultural Exchange Programmes (CEPs) and other collaborative arrangements, and monitoring of the educational component of the bilateral and collaborative programmes with other countries.

The INC has been closely associated with the work of the Delors Commission on Education for the 21st Century. The Report of the Commission, Learning: The Treasure Within, has been reprinted by the INC for wider dissemination. A national debate is envisaged on the recommendations of the Report. A two-member delegation of the Department also attended the Conference on Education for the 21st Century in the Asia-Pacific Region, held at Melbourne from 30 March to 3 April, 1998. The Bilateral Exchange Programmes connected with the university sector, between India and other countries, are implemented by the UGC on behalf of the Government of India. In 1996-97, such programmes had been initiated with 70 countries.

Development of bilateral linkages in specific areas between identified departments of universities and institutions of higher education have been given greater emphasis. The UGC provides foreign language teachers to universities having a proper infrastructure for teaching foreign languages under the Collaborative Exchange Programmes. In 1996-97, 32 foreign teachers in German, French, Chinese, Portuguese, Spanish, Hungarian, Mongolian, Iranian, Russian, Polish, Rumanian, Pushto and Korean were assigned to various universities in India. Several scholarships and fellowships have been instituted in Indian universities with the support of the German and French governments. The UGC also implements the scheme of SAARC Chairs/Fellowships/Scholarships.

An Academic Link Interchange Scheme is being implemented in collaboration with the British Council for the development of linkages between institutions in higher education in India and the UK, in specific areas such as joint research, joint publication, curriculum development and so on. Under the Commonwealth Academic Staff Fellowships/Scholarships programme, the UGC coordinates with the Association of Commonwealth Universities (ACU) in UK and makes nominations for the award of Commonwealth fellowships and scholarships to enable promising faculty members in universities and colleges in India to do research work at the universities/ institutions in the UK. Proposals from 13 Universities for undertaking the Canadian Studies programme have been approved by the UGC. Financial support is being provided to these universities, at various levels, for undertaking studies relating to the historical, social, economic and political aspects of Canada. Travel grants are provided by the UGC for teachers who have offers of fellowships/stipends for foreign countries for collection of source material for their research work.

VISION AND TASKS AHEAD

India realizes, like other nations of the world, that humanity stands today at the head of a new age of a large synthesis of knowledge, and that the East and the West have to collaborate in bringing about concerted action for universal upliftment, and lasting peace and unity. In this new age, great cultural achievements of the past have to be recovered and enriched in the context of the contemporary advancement so that humanity can successfully meet the evolutionary and revolutionary challenges and bring about a new type of humanity and society marked by integrated powers of physical, emotional, dynamic, intellectual, ethical, aesthetic and spiritual potentialities. Frontiers of knowledge are, therefore, bound to expand unimaginably, and new researches will oblige humanities, sciences, technologies, and fine arts to arrive at new equations and new combinations.

All these factors will impel higher education to undergo vast changes in respect of objectives, contents and methods. It will have to bear momentous responsibilities for generating new vistas of knowledge and wisdom, bolder forms of courage and heroism, unprecedented arts of harmony and beauty, and unimaginable skills suited to developing technologies and crafts. It will also be required to set more exacting standards of excellence and perfection.

Information Age

The world is entering into an Information Age and developments in communication, information and technology will open up new and cost-effective approaches for providing the reach of higher education to the youth as well as to those who need continuing education for meeting the demands of explosion of information, fast-changing nature of occupations, and lifelong education.

We also feel called upon to encourage and support the forces and developments relating to the learning society and to the theme of the sovereignty of learners, particularly young people. India has already decided to launch "Operation Knowledge" as a part of the Information Technology Action Plan. This will mean not only continuous expansion and improvement of the facilities of modern equipment but also a gigantic task to redesign teaching-learning materials in every discipline appropriate to the special demands of the new technologies and media of transmission and new teacher-pupil relations.

A most difficult task ahead is to conceive certain new objectives of higher education. It will not be enough to promote specialized knowledge and skills of professional excellence; a deeper and subtler aim will be to develop abilities to think globally and to resolve emerging tensions between rationa-listic, ethical, aesthetic and spiritual elements of personality. The objective of a complete education for a complete human being will need to be underlined as of highest importance.

Another major task will be to change the contents of higher education. Appropriate courses have to be designed so as to achieve a proper blending of wide general knowledge and such specialization, which would have in-built facilities to renew relevant knowledge and skills at increasingly shorter intervals and even on a continuous basis. Increasing freedom of choice in selecting subjects of studies has to be ensured, and interdisciplinary studies will have to be so devised that they will foster understanding and appreciation of national history in the context of the goal of multicultural under-standing and of creating in the world a harmonious human family, appropriate to the ancient Indian ideal of "Vasudhaiva Kutumbakam".

Methods of higher education also have to be appropriate to the needs of learning to learn, learning to do, learning to be and learning to become. Student-centred education and employment of dynamic methods of education will require from teachers new attitudes and new skills. Methods of teaching through lectures will have to subordinated to the methods that will lay stress on self-study, personal consultation between teachers and pupils, and dynamic sessions of seminars and workshops. Methods of distance education will have to be employed on a vast scale.

Teachers - New Dimensions of their Role

Special emphasis on value-oriented education will impart a new dimension to the role of the teacher. For value-orientation cannot be imparted without teachers' own value-orientation. Again, the objective of integral development of personality cannot be fulfilled without teachers developing their own integral personality. It is increasingly recognized that if the defences of peace are to be built in the minds of men and women, and if the qualities of cooperation, mutuality and harmony are to be fostered in humanity, the role of the teacher will include the task of changing the tendencies of egoism and domination that are the ultimate causes of division and war. It is particularly for this reason that a new programme of teaches' training has to be envisaged, and this programme will not only cater to the continuous development of professional skills but also continuous development of teachers' ethical and spiritual abilities.

Appropriate to the new and difficult demands on teachers, we have to constantly raise the status of teachers in the country. India recognizes that access to higher education will have to be so broad-based that the system of open universities has to continue to grow and it will not only have to be extended vastly but also to be so designed that it can foster among students constant motivation to learn and to develop not only academic abilities but also practical skills and talents that are being demanded by the modern world.

A major task ahead is to bring about radical changes in the system of examination. Methods of testing have to be so devised that not only will tests be rigorous but they will be so flexible and of varied nature so as to be appropriate to the demands of promoting various curricular and non-curricular abilities, physical fitness, artistic taste, and value-orientation. The new testing system should facilitate delinking of degrees from jobs and curricular reforms bringing in emphasis on multi-disciplinary courses. Such changes will also be a recognition of the sovereignty of the learner and of making education reality-oriented and learner-centred.

Towards a Learning Society

As we move towards a learning society, every human activity will require contributions from experts, and this will place the entire sector of higher education in sharp focus. Although the priorities, which are being assigned today to the task of Education for All, will continue to be preponderant, the country will have to prepare itself to invest more and more on higher education and, simultaneously, measures will have to be taken to refine, diversify and upgrade higher education and research programmes. Our present system of governance of higher education is undergoing increasing strain, and sooner rather than later, major changes will have to be effected not only to ensure greater autonomy and accountability but also to facilitate rapid changes in the very framework, directions and goals.

Financial strain in the educational sector imposes several difficult tasks not only relating to fee structure and new partnership of education with industry and various income and profit generating sectors but also to the cost-effective designs of structures and methodologies of education that can cater to the needs of massive programmes of education as also to those of intensive education that aim at individual perfection. The advances in communication technology, specially the satellite based teleconferencing, have made it possible to use distance education for training skills in virtual classrooms. It is expected that technology, rightly designed for developing deeper and higher dimensions of personality, will at once bring down the costs and increase the efficiency of the educational system.

Realistic Optimism

India looks upon the future with realistic optimism, despite difficult challenges and world-wide crises through which humanity is passing today. We feel that major efforts are required to cross over the present transitional period, during which negative forces will try to outweigh the positive forces. But considering the vast ethical and spiritual potentialities that lie really untapped, we can trust that humanity will overcome the crisis and emerge stronger to create a new world of harmony and unity. But in fulfilling this hope, education will have to play a crucial role. Considering also that future advances in research will affect the theme of higher knowledge centrally, the country is getting ready to strengthen the system of higher education and to adopt strategies that will provide new dimensions to the delivery system that will help change society and prepare young people to shoulder the heavy responsibilities of a difficult but fascinating future.

8

EDUCATIONAL CHALLENGES IN INDIA

CHALLENGES OF PRIMARY EDUCATION

Early childhood education in India is subject to two extreme but contrary deficiencies. On the one hand, millions of young children in lower income groups, especially rural and girl children, comprising nearly 40% of first grade entrants never complete primary school. Even among those who do, poorly qualified teachers, very high student-teacher ratios, inadequate teaching materials and out-moded teaching methods result in a low quality of education that often imparts little or no real learning. It is not uncommon for students completing six years of primary schooling in village public schools to lack even rudimentary reading and writing skills.

At the other end of the social and educational spectrum, children attending urban schools, especially middle and upper class children in private schools, are subjected to extreme competitive pressures from a very early age to acquire basic language skills and memorize vast amounts of information in order to qualify for admission into the best schools.

Parents and teachers exert intense pressure on young children to acquire academic skills at an age when children should be given freedom and encouraged to learn as a natural outcome of their innate curiosity, playfulness and eagerness to experiment. Rising concern over compulsory learning at an early age is prompting many educators to advocate dramatic steps to counter the obsession with premature and forced teaching practices.

Between these two extreme positions, lie a wide array of mostly mediocre practices. Rarely do we find the educational system fostering the natural process of spontaneous, self-motivated self-education in which children learn just as they play and as a form of play out of their innate curiosity and urge to acquire knowledge of the environment. Internationally, there have been many efforts to find a 'third way' that suffers neither from the sad neglect all too common in low quality public education or the compulsive pressures exerted even on very young children by competitive, career-conscious school systems.

A highly successful alternative approach has been evolved in the USA by the Institute for the Development of Human Potential, founded by the eminent educationist Dr. Glenn Doman. Doman's work is founded upon the conviction that learning is a natural instinctive urge in young children that is very often curbed or destroyed either by neglect and lack of exposure or by compulsory teaching. During more than three decades of work with both normal and brain damaged children, Doman has shown that exposing young children to interesting sources of information for very brief periods each day actually stimulates the development of the brain cells during early years and fosters a spontaneous curiosity and natural love of learning in children. Doman's methods have been practiced for more than 20 years at the Institute's school in Philadelphia and more recently in similar institutions established in South America, Western Europe and Japan. The same methods have been applied successfully by more than one million parents around the world.

Another alternative approach has been evolved and practiced for the past 45 years at the Sri Aurobindo International

Centre of Education in Pondicherry. Here too the emphasis has been on fostering a conducive atmosphere for the children's curiosity to emerge and express itself so that they acquire a natural inclination toward learning and self-development.

SHISHAYATAN SCHOOL

The Anugriha Charitable Trust was established in 1993 by Mr. and Mrs. R. Raghavan as a public charitable trust with the intention of evolving and demonstrating alternative educational methods in India. The Trust is registered under section 11 & 12 of the Indian Income Tax Act and exempted under section 80G. Mr. Raghavan is a chartered accountant and computer consultant who established and operated a consulting firm in Bombay before leaving the city to establish a rural school in Tamil Nadu. Aruna Raghavan is an M.Phil in English, a former sub-editor of a reputed English magazine and former teacher at the Kodaikanal International School, Gandhi Vidyashram and a high school in Bombay. The Raghavans have spent the last decade exploring and experimenting with new methods of early childhood education.

In 1991 they established the Primrose Institute in Bombay where they conducted courses for parents on how to utilize alternative educational methods to foster a love of learning in their own. In 1992 the Raghavans left Bombay and invested their entire savings to establish a primary school at Arasavanangkadu, a village of 1500 people situated ten kilometers from Kumbakonam in Tamil Nadu. The school commenced operations in mid 1994 admitting 15 children aged 3 - 3 to the first class. All of the children were drawn from low income, scheduled caste families in which they are the first generation to receive any education.

The system of education provided at the Arasavanangkadu School is based on the following approach:

— The most important aspect of the approach is attitude of the teacher, which should be that learning is a form of play which fosters the blossoming of the child's natural development. Learning should and can be made interesting, enjoyable, fun.

— A large portion of the teaching materials are produced at the school by the teachers, who customize their teaching aids to suit the interests and knowledge levels of the students.

— First attention is given to the health and nutrition of the children to ensure that they have the physical energy and natural attention span needed for learning. Nutritional and medical supplements are provided to under nourished children from low income families. Free exercising and play are encouraged to build strength and stamina.

— Children learn spontaneously when their interest and curiosity are awakened. 'Teaching' is confined to brief periods according to the natural attention span of each child, which is normally 15-30 minutes daily during the first two years. It is never extended beyond the child's span of interest.

— The student-teacher ratio is kept very low to enable the teacher to work with small groups of 4-5 children at a time while the others are absorbed in learning games or recreational play. The most effective ratio is five students per teacher during pre-school, LKG and HKG and twenty students per teacher during standards 1 to 5. However, since the teaching methods are intense, each student actually need attend only 2 to 3 hours of class per day, enabling each teacher to effectively handle double the number of students.

— The act of teaching consists primarily of presenting sensory images, objects and information to the child in a pleasant and interesting manner and permitting the child to observe and inquire about the subject, without compelling the child to memorize. Coloured flash cards with large images are utilized as convenient, low cost teaching aids.

— Rapid acquisition of basic reading and verbal skills in multiple languages occurs naturally by exposing the child to whole words as objects repetitively for very brief periods. In this manner at a young age even children of illiterate parents learn several languages as effortlessly as they normally learn to speak their native tongue.

— Story telling is used to make learning fun and to communicate basic values of goodness, beauty, harmony, responsibility and right conduct.

— Information on people and other living things, places, history, geography, and other cultures are presented to the child in the form of stories, pictorial information and explanations combined together to present facts in a living, integrated context rather than as a series of separate divorced subjects.

— Rapid acquisition of basic math skills is achieved through the use of number line method which enables the child to physically experiment and act out different combinations of addition and subtraction.

First Year Results

— Most of the children come to the school so underdeveloped and under-nourished that almost exclusive emphasis is placed during the first 3-6 months on providing nutritional supplements and free exercise to develop motor skills.

— As the children gained health and strength, their attention span and curiosity have increase to the point where they happily explore new learning areas for periods from 15 to 30 minutes per day.

— Despite the very brief time exposure, very average children are able to read simple Tamil and English stories by the end of 15 months.

— During the same period, they also learn to recognize all the states of India, the geography of the country, the continents, peoples of the world and a wide range of plant and animal species.

— In addition to teaching the children, the school also engaged two unemployed women from the village with teaching credentials and successfully trained in these methods. The trainees have learned and now regularly apply these methods for teaching our children and they also actively participate in the design of lessons and production of the teaching materials.

— Although there was initial skepticism and suspicion from the village community, including the families of the first year children, parents have become proud of their children and the village as a whole has come to embrace the school. Requests for admission are coming from villages in a ten mile radius.

These results can be compared with the learning of children from comparable backgrounds attending the local public school, most of whom are unable to read and understand even Tamil sentences at the end of six years of primary education.

Over the past two decades, similar methods have been tested and proven effective in homes and schools in many different countries and social environments around the world. The effort at Shishayatan demonstrates that these same methods can be successfully applied even in the most challenging context working with disadvantaged children of uneducated, illiterate poor parents, many of whom question the value of any education whatsoever based on the experience of children attending public schools in the area.

The Trust plans to expand the school each year to take in new students at pre-school level and progressively add classes up to and through the eighth standard. This will require a gradual expansion of the teaching staff and addition of new classrooms each year. The school has demonstrated that it is possible to teach this educational method to suitably qualified young adults from the rural community and that once taught they display very positive attitudes and good teaching skill in working with the children.

Objectives

The aim of this proposal is to outline effective strategies by which the education system practiced at Shishayatan can be tested and extended to all parts of India.

This aim can be achieved provided that following conditions are met:

1. The pioneering work of the Arasavanangkadu School has to be extended up to the fifth standard over the next five years to demonstrate that even disadvantaged children from rural families can acquire educational levels normally that normally require ten years or more of study, even in urban schools, and that this can be accomplished by encouraging the natural curiosity of the child rather than through the pressure and forced learning patterns common in highly competitive urban schools. This will require expansion of the existing school to accept larger numbers of students and add additional classes, so that total student enrollment at Shishayatan reaches 150-200 students by the end of five years.
2. A training institute should be established to train teachers and trainers in the methods employed at the school, so that those trained can serve as a nucleus for establishing new schools and as a means of inducting these teaching methods into existing schools the country.
3. It is essential to build public awareness and acceptance of this approach to early child education, so that existing schools will be willing to experiment with the new methods and so that new schools will be favorable received by the community. This can be achieved through a combination of media educational programmes and demonstration projects carried out in established schools around the country.
4. Financial resources will need to be raised to support expansion of the Arasavanangkadu School and for establishment of the training institute.

5. The special teaching and course material employed by these methods must be reproduced on a sufficiently large and economical scale to support widespread dissemination.
6. Existing schools should be identified that are willing to incorporate these teaching methods as part of their normal educational programme and new pre- and primary schools should be established based entirely on these methods.

EDUCATIONAL POLICY OF INDIA

The Government of India's National Policy on Education, 1986 (modified in the year 1992) is a forthright statement on Education as an empowering agent. The country has reached a stage in its economic and technical development where a major effort must be made to derive maximum benefit from the assets already created and to ensure that the fruits of development reach all sections. The NPE, thus, rightly identified for focussed attention and intervention, a number of thrust areas which inter-alia included education for equality at all stages of education, open learning systems, promoting efficiency and effectiveness at all levels and making the system work through effective management of education.

The Central Government while making certain modifications in NPE (1986) in 1992 took a significant decision to direct the State Governments to have their own State Programme of Action for implementing the thrust areas of the policy in view of local conditions keeping the spirit of NPE intact. The State of Haryana also devised its own State POA in 1994. The NPE further provided for a periodic review of the thrust areas in consonance with the dynamics of education related needs and aspirations of the populace. Hence the need now to identify new areas of action & take suitable policy initiatives.

At the threshold of the new millennium, the Government of Haryana has sought to address the challenges thrown up by the changing environment and the problems being faced by the state in terms of key HRD indicators by bringing Education at the central stage of its development agenda.

At this stage of development, the education agenda of the state requires re-negotiation from quantity to quality, from mere transfer of information to enhancement of creativity & knowledge and development of relevant skills, from a centralized to a decentralized system of educational administration and from bureaucratic management to a participative decision making process. The overall objective is to make education relevant to the emerging environment by way of encouraging socially & economically productive skills.

Haryana, which was carved out of the erstwhile Punjab in 1966, had come into existence as a deprived and underdeveloped state. The efforts of the people of the State and the Govt have led to a stage, where Haryana has the distinction of having the third highest per capita income. Haryana has made commendable progress in many areas on the economic front, like providing electricity, metalled roads and potable water to all the villages besides giving thrust to industries alongwith technical and material inputs in agriculture. The life expectancy and per capita income of the state have risen considerably. During the same period the literacy rate has risen to 55.85% as compared to the national average of 52.21% (1991 census). This has to be viewed in the context of the fact that in 1966 at the time of reorganisation the State's literacy rate (19.92%, Census 1961) was lower than the national average (27.76%, Census 1961).

Despite the major strides made by Haryana, the State ranks among the lowest in the country in many of the HRD indicators. For instance, the birth rate in the State remains higher than the national average and far above the replacement level. During 1981-91 the sex ratio between males and females has gone down from 878 to 865 and is the lowest in the country. Although, the enrolment of girls has improved since the inception of the state, yet it remains low. The drop-out rate among girls in the elementary stage is high and the percentage of girls going for education at the secondary and college stage is low.

At the time of initial thrust for universalisation of elementary education, there was voluntary community participation. Most of the schools in the rural areas were made by the panchayats or the communities and the land for the schools was given free of cost by the panchayats. The efforts of the State at universalisation of elementary education increased the coverage extensively, yet, it led to a system of centralization at the cost of community participation. Today the community and the panchayats stand alienated from the monolithic educational infrastructure that has evolved in the State.

Although it is a matter of great satisfaction that enrolment of children has crossed the 90% mark (private schools enrolment included), and accessibility of schools has improved considerably, yet, many of the disadvantaged and weaker sections and physically and mentally challenged groups have largely remained outside the ambit of elementary education. In order to achieve universalisation of elementary education, the needs of these special groups will have to be addressed. Any further progress in increasing the percentage of enrolment would necessarily demand that education is made accessible to these sections by making it more relevant and flexible as per their requirements.

Recognizing the child's fundamental right to education, serious thought would also need to be given to the question of making appropriate provisions in the Constitution so that full benefits of the UEE are derived by the 6-14 years age group.

Although the percentage of girls getting enrolled in the schools has gone up in the last three decades, yet the drop-out rate among them remains high. The number of girls going for higher or professional education is still very small. Special efforts need to be made to increase the access of higher education for this section.

After having reached a satisfactory degree of universalisation of elementary education, the State is now concerned about the quality of education. Whereas the content of what is taught is important, equally important is the efficacy of the delivery system and the teaching technologies. Effective management of education to ensure optimum returns is therefore an area to be urgently addressed.

Any further progress, even on the economic front, will only be possible by increased expenditure on education. Examples from other developing countries have shown that the growth of the economy is directly related to the educational levels. The growth rate of economy in Haryana is slowing down while the growth rate of economy in the southern states, where education levels are better, is picking up. The Planning Commission has recommended an expenditure of 6% of the GDP on education. The state of Haryana, since its inception, has had major obligations towards meeting basic needs of the people and development of the infrastructure. As such, it has only been able to allocate up to 2.1% of the state GDP for education. A paradigm shift is required in the allocation of resources for education which should ideally reach 6% of the GDP. Private initiative must play an equally important role in the field of education. The private and government initiative should go hand in hand in a participative manner.

In the field of higher education , the private initiative is certainly greater as there are more private colleges than government colleges. Yet, over a period of time the dependence of the private institutions on government resources has increased to an extent where 95% of the deficit of private colleges is being met by the state exchequer. If we are to encourage private initiative in higher education, then it would be appropriate to devise methods and systems whereby the coverage of these institutions increases without accompanying additional expenditure on the state exchequer. Strategies will have to be evolved to allow a degree of greater autonomy to these institutions so that the support of the state resources is no longer necessary.

When a review of educational scenario of the state is done in the year 2000, we cannot close our eyes to the emerging socio-economic scenario in the country and the world. Major technological advances have been made, especially in the field of information technology. The liberalized economic environment in the country since 1991 has made India porous to the new developments in the outside world. Severe competition is emerging in the industrial world. Continuous innovation is the key to competitive advantage in the modern world of trade and commerce, making rapid obsolence of skills a major challenge. In such an emerging environment education needs to be made more relevant to the environment. A necessary thrust has to be generated in the field of vocationalisation of education and introduction of courses aimed at imparting the required skills including Information Technology. The problem of rapid obsolence of skills would have to be additionally addressed through programmes of Continuing Education.

In view of new areas of concern having evolved over the last few years in the State of Haryana, it has been felt that there is a need to reorient the thrust of education policy. It has been the endeavour of the State Govt. to involve policy makers, educational administrators , academicians and other stakeholders in the process of setting the educational agenda. There have been statewide debates and workshops at various levels involving educationists and community leaders which have resulted in giving direction to the State's Education Policy 2000.

POLICY OBJECTIVES

— The State Govt. shall accord topmost priority to Universalisation of Elementary Education and take all necessary steps to achieve this objective by the year 2005.

— The State Govt. shall support the endeavour of Govt. of India to declare elementary education a fundamental right of the child besides amendments in Article 51 of the Constitution enjoining upon the parents the fundamental duty of sending their children to schools.

— The State shall strive towards achieving a substantial increase in both public and private investments in education so that the public investment goes upto 6% of GDP by the year 2010 A.D. and the total investment including private investment goes upto 10% of the GDP in the same period.

— The State Govt. shall take effective steps to encourage transfer of elementary educational institution to the PRIs and the Urban Local Bodies in a bid to empower the community and other stake holders.

— The State shall elicit active participation of Village Education Committees, Mother Teacher Associations, Parent Teacher Associations in management of education.

— The State shall promote NGOs to play a key role in the qualitative and quantitative expansion of education.

— The State shall focus on reducing disparities based on gender, region, class, category including children of special focus groups etc. Based on the principle of equality and social justice, it will aim at creating an appropriate environment which allows and encourages children including girls, special and challenged children to develop their full potential and contribute to the nation's growth.

— Recognising the central role of teachers in education, the State reposes its full faith and trust in teachers and will support them in improving their knowledge and skills in pedagogy and child- oriented learning. With a view to keeping abreast the teachers with the latest developments in education and to upgrade their professional skills at regular intervals, the existing training programmes will be further strengthened besides, introducing pre-induction training for both school and college teachers.

— The State shall endeavour to reorient the educational system so as to make it holistic, qualitative, socially and economically productive and relevant to the fast changing socio- economic environment. Emphasis would be laid on acquisition of relevant knowledge, skills and values and their application to real life situations.

— The State shall take effective steps to minimize wastages and enhance productivity in education. This would include efficient management of resources, review of teaching methodologies, updation of course curriculum, review of evaluation system etc.

— Education shall be merit driven. Recruitments / appointments, promotions, postings, transfers, deployments shall all be based on merit alone within the overall frame work of the state policy.

— The State shall strengthen the teacher-institution link and discourage dislocations.

— The State Shall introduce computer education at school and college levels to translate into action the I.T. policy.

— Keeping in view the demands of globalization of economy and advent of information technology, the State Govt. shall endeavour to link education with the world at work and would help in the multi-dimensional growth of all sections of the society. The State Govt. shall accord priority to the introduction of vocational, I.T., technical, need-based courses in higher education.

— As a step towards removal of rural-urban disparities among students at the elementary level and to equip them with the necessary linguistics skills, English shall be introduced in all primary schools from class I.

— The State Govt. shall lay emphasis on consolidation/ optimum utilization of existing infrastructure/facilities in education, quality improvement, education mapping and conferment of autonomous status to deserving institutions of higher education Rural areas will get special attention.

— For policy planning, coordination as also for maintaining academic standards in higher education, the State Govt. shall endeavour to establish the State Council for Higher Education as a statutory body. The State shall endeavour to make the teachers training institutions autonomous.

— With a view to providing necessary freedom for innovation and creating a climate to meet futuristic demands, the State

Govt. shall encourage private investment, self-financ... higher education.

— Suitable mechanisms for enhancing accountability at all levels shall be evolved and adherence to a code of professional ethics enforced.

— The State Govt. shall endeavour to bring about certain changes in the management structure of higher education with a view to having close linkages between primary, middle, secondary, senior secondary and higher education.

— Reforms in examination and evaluation system is a continuous process. Fast changing education scenario also poses a challenge for higher education necessitating periodic review of courses, curriculum, examination etc. The State Govt. shall advise the State Universities to have an inbuilt mechanism to address these areas.

— As a part of recognizing merit and promoting excellence, the State shall endeavour to honour best institutions, meritorious students, best teachers and best heads of institutions.

— The State shall endeavour to make NCC, NSS, sports, value education, environmental education, yoga, scouting etc. as an integral part of institutional activities.

— With a view to augmenting opportunities for education, ensuring access at door step to different sections of the society, bringing flexibility and making education a life long process, the State Govt. shall endeavour to encourage/ strengthen existing facilities in distance/open-learning systems.

IMPLEMENTATION STRATEGIES

School as a planning unit :- Schools would be strengthened as institutions in order to make them truly effective. The school shall be a full fledged institutional entity with its own goals and plans & not a mere recipient of orders from "above". Consequently, planning and management at the level of schools would be encouraged.

...ralisation of Educational Administration:- The state ...endeavour to decentralise the educational system in such a way that it empowers the stakeholders and the Panchayati Raj Institutions and urban local bodies. In general, the participation of parents, communities and grass root level local bodies will be encouraged through formation of Village Education Committees / Village Construction Committees. These committees shall be constituted by necessary amendments in the Panchayati Raj Act and the Municipal Act and empowered to undertake repair & maintenance work as also additions and alterations to the tune of Rs. 1.25 lacs on each work.

The school would be viewed as embedded in the community. A continuous, mutually supportive school - community interaction / dialogue would be encouraged. The processes of micro-planning and community mobilization would strengthen the school-community link. Formation of bodies such as Village Education Committees in villages would create community ownership of the school and generate community support for it.

Attempts to strengthen the school as an institution would be accompanied by parallel changes in the existing district and sub-district level administrative structure. Appropriate changes would therefore be made at the district and sub-district level so as to reorient the present administrative system to be responsive to the needs of the school, have respect for the autonomy of the school, and play a supportive rather than punitive role.

Quality in delivery of primary education :- The emphasis will now be on improving quality of education being imparted in the schools . Improved and child-friendly text books, Teaching Learning Materials, Action Research by the practising teachers to identify hard-spots in learning, improving the system of lesson- transaction within the class room will form the thrust areas in the field of pedagogical improvement. The approach will include the various pedagogy related inputs in a comprehensive way based on locally defined needs and field realities. The practising teachers would be involved in the process of pedagogical change, revival and renewal. Solutions would be arrived at locally. The school will become the focal point providing the requisite growth environment not only for the students but also the teachers.

Introduction of English from class-I :- To prepare children particularly in rural areas to face and meet the challenges thrown up by the changing environment, English will be introduced as a subject from class -I. The existing staff would be trained and oriented to shoulder this new responsibility. The endeavour would be to encourage multi-grade teaching under situations where there is a paucity of teachers.

Capacity Building of teachers :- Besides in-service training, induction and in-school training would be introduced. Training would be need-prompted and based on feed back received from the schools. The talents and aptitudes of teachers would be collated to promote their inherent talents through training. The practising teachers will be encouraged to associate themselves with pedagogical work and researches.

Effective linkages will be established between the schools and DIETs and SCERT which would be suitably strengthened and made autonomous so as to be able to play a more meaningful role in the drive for pedagogical revival in the State. The whole approach to training and manpower development will be motivational and inspirational as well as participative.

Strengthening the teacher-school link :- A new transfer policy will be evolved to ensure that rural schools in backward areas do not remain without teachers while at the same time making the whole issue of transfers more transparent, fair and equitable for the teaching community. All teachers would compulsorily do a five year stint in rural schools on first appointment. Transfers shall be an exception and not the rule. No teacher shall be dislocated before five years in a particular school except for administrative exigencies.

Recognition of teachers :-Due recognition will be provided to outstanding and dedicated teachers in the form of rewards and their academic growth and development shall be given special attention. The objective would be to promote Intellect and Integrity. The role of the head of the institution in schools and colleges shall be reasserted. Besides, best institutions, best teachers and the best heads of institutions would be given due recognition. A special incentive scheme would be introduced for villages attaining UPE, UEE and total literacy.

Community mobilisation and support :- Community mobilization will not be confined to merely encouraging the community to provide finances for creating physical assets at the village level. Nor will this mean the interpolation of another inspectoral/ supervisory level in the administrative hierarchy of education. It would mean involving and enlisting the support of the community as partners in the process of change happening in the schools.

The community would be fully involved on all issues relating to developing the school plan for the village, understanding the problems of the girl child as well as issues of retention and repetition in the school in their village, providing health and nutrition support which is a form of learning preparedness for the children in the village. The village education committees will provide the window between the schools and the community. Village enrolment registers, health registers as well as the routing of incentives and scholarships will be maintained and done through the VECs.

Thus, there will be a paradigm shift from a welfare approach where the villagers are seen as passive recipients to a development approach where the village community is an equal partner in the process of change. Recognising the role that women can play in the education of their children, mother-teacher associations would be encouraged in addition to PTAs.

Mainstreaming Special Focus Groups :- The State will also recognize the unique problems that special focus groups of children face, requiring convergence with other departments. Accordingly, Alternate Schools will be started for the yet unreached girl-child with her home as the central place, for the street and working child who does not have a place to call a home, for the mentally and physically challenged child whose problems are rather unique. Under the Education Policy, the aim would be to ultimately main-stream these children from the Alternate Schools to regular schools.

Learning packages will be developed to provide for open-ended entry and exit for such children as well as to take care of the educational needs of these children based upon their individual difficulties. In its effort to synergise the activities of the education department with other departments, anganwadis would be located in primary schools wherever space is available so that the system of having nursery classes in rural areas is also given shape. The ICDS workers will devote extra time to the educational requirements of such pre-school children and there will be a functional linkage between the primary school teachers and the ICDS workers.

Monitoring and Evaluation :- Collation of data would take place on a continuing basis at the grass-root level. This would enable higher offices to have a variety of informed choices before embarking upon any policy initiatives. To familiar proper analysis and use of the of data so generated, the district and block level offices and also the head office would be computerized.

Increased Allocation/Resource Mobilization for Education:- The state shall endeavour to increase the allocation of funds for education from the present 2.1% of the state GDP to 6.0% of the state GDP by the year 2010 as recommended by the Planning Commission. The state shall in addition endeavour to encourage private initiative so as to take the total allocation of resources to 10% during the same period.

The State would acknowledge the role of the private sector as well as the community in owning up the responsibility of taking up the issue of educating the masses. With growing economic power, alternative options have started evolving and people in the rural areas have started sending their children to private schools. The government would not see the private initiative as competition. Rather, the Government would try to improve the quality of education in Government schools to bring these schools at par with private schools wherever such a necessity exists. However, the Government would regulate conditions to discourage an exploitative environment in private schools.

The State would encourage registration of college level societies comprising parents, Principals, elected representatives, social workers, alumni, Govt. representatives etc. Such societies would be empowered to raise resources and incur expenditure for the development of colleges in areas such as infrastructure, student/staff amenities, equipment etc. in colleges.

Retention of Girl Students :- In order to retain the girl students in the schools and to encourage enrolment of girls in the Colleges, there are certain special needs specific to this section which need to be addressed. The state shall endeavour to strengthen the necessary infrastructure in both schools and colleges which will encourage retention of girls in the schools and increase enrolment in colleges.

Introduction of IT in Education:- The state shall introduce Computer Education in schools, both urban & rural, at appropriate levels to prepare the next generation to face the challenges thrown up by globalisation of economy and establishment of information highways. Subject to availability of resources, the state shall endeavour to introduce Computers as aids in education at the elementary level also, for better appreciation of the subjects taught. In addition to the usual courses in Colleges, the state shall endeavour to introduce Certificate / Diploma / Degree Courses in Computer Applications of relevance to the Industry.

Vocational Education:- The state shall endeavour to make the curriculum relevant to the changing socio-economic environment and strengthen the vocational education at the

10+2 level. In addition the State shall consider introduction of relevant subjects like Agriculture, Home Science, Animal Husbandry and other socially productive areas as compulsory or elective subjects at appropriate levels.

In an effort to supplement UGC sponsored vocational courses, the State Govt. shall allow Govt. and Non-Govt. Colleges to start vocational, technical, need-based courses under self financing scheme. Short term vocational courses shall also be allowed to be introduced in the evenings.

Replication of gains of DPEP:- The Programmes of DPEP-I & DPEP-II funded by the World Bank, in seven districts of the state have yielded commendable results. It shall be the endeavour of the state to sustain the gains of the DPEP and replicate them in the whole state, to the extent possible.

Optimum Utilisation of Infrastructure: - The state shall endeavour to optimise utilisation of existing infrastructure in schools and colleges by way of introducing shift system wherever required, and utilise the buildings for open learning courses in the evening.

Making Higher Education Relevant & removing disparities :- The State shall introduce courses in emerging areas of education including vocational, technical, Information Technology etc. linking higher education with the world at work. The State will take initiative to encourage private investment in higher education for diversification of courses in urban areas, expansion of facilities in rural areas and qualitative improvements. Linkages will be established with off shore universities of repute and the industries to make courses respond to the fast changing demands of the market.

Remedial Coaching:- In addition to UGC sponsored scheme of remedial coaching both for annual examinations as well as for competitive examinations for students from focussed groups, the State Govt. shall broadbase the programme departmentally so as to cover all educational institutions in the State.

Autonomy:- With a view to providing freedom in designing courses, innovation, research etc. the State Govt. will take all necessary steps to confer autonomy on colleges having the potential to grow as centres of excellence.

Pre-induction and in-service training for college teachers :- Pre-induction training would be designed and imparted to newly appointed lecturers before they actually take up the teaching assignment. Human Resource Development would be a major thrust area involving intensive in-service training of teachers to enable them to grow and upgrade their knowledge and skills.

Open learning & distance education :- In order to realize the goal of education , as also to provide education at the door step to those who are not able to join regular courses , open-learning/distance education shall be strengthened.

Empowering women and focussed groups :- The State Govt. shall endeavour to empower women and focussed groups by strengthening existing network of Women Studies and Development Cells functioning in the colleges, expansion of hostel facilities for girls, remedial coaching, gender awareness programmes and gender sensitive curriculum.

Establishing State Council for Higher Education :- For planning and coordination of higher education as also for maintaining standards, the State Govt. shall endeavour to establish State Council for Higher Education as a statutory body.

Based on above implementation strategies, a detailed POA (Programme of Action) shall be prepared by the departments of Primary, Secondary and Higher Education to implement the policy objectives enlisted in the Education Policy for the State of Haryana, 2000 within the overall framework of National Policy on Education, 1986 (as amended in 1992).

INDEX